Do You Want to Be Healed?

DO YOU WANT
TO BE HEALED?

by John Sutherland Bonnell

HARPER AND ROW, PUBLISHERS

NEW YORK, EVANSTON, AND LONDON

1817

TO

My Friend
REGINALD AUCHINCLOSS, PH.D.

FIRST EDITION

LIBRARY OF CONGRESS CATALOG CARD NUMBER: 68-31161

Preface

Tʜɪs ʙᴏᴏᴋ has been four years in preparation. During this time I have had conferences and conversations on the subject of spiritual healing with both religious and medical leaders in countries on four continents of the world: Australia, India, Great Britain, France, Italy and the United States. The high points of these conversations were visits with Harley Street physicians in London and conferences with physicians and church leaders at the Shrine of Lourdes in France. Two and one half years spent in training as a psychiatric nurse in a Canadian mental hospital and more than eight thousand pastoral sessions on all manner of human ills was a most helpful preparation for the medical conferences. One has only to read such a book as A History of the Warfare of Science with Theology in Christendom[1] to see that the medical profession, having got rid of most of its superstitions, had a stiff fight to free itself from the enthrallments of false religious concepts. This conflict has left scars that are slow to heal.

Happily, we have now entered upon an era of genuine cooperation and mutual understanding between a trained clergy and doctors. In the hospitals of America from time to time physicians gladly avail themselves of the services of hospital chaplains, and the assistance

[1] Dr. Andrew W. White (New York: D. Appleton and Co., 1897); 2 vols.

of competent parish ministers is frequently sought by family doctors.

In citing instances of healing in this book I have deliberately refrained from reporting anything savoring of startling cases of recovery from organic diseases. This is not because the evidence for these happenings is inconclusive, but because they occur very infrequently in the ministry even of those who have had most success in this field. Let it not be forgotten that only sixty-two cases of miraculous physical healings have been reported by Lourdes throughout a period of more than one hundred years.

Our greatest need at this time is to bring the healing power of God to bear upon the lives of countless thousands of persons who are overborne by the burdens and problems of life. This will entail a recovery of the commission our Lord gave to his Apostles and followers to heal as well as to proclaim the gospel. The historic churches especially have been sadly lacking at this point. It will avail little to their parishioners if the pastors deplore the extremes and garish publicity attending the ministry of "faith healers" and yet themselves have nothing whatsoever to offer. Our ministry must be to the minds and souls of our people as well as to their bodies. Dr. Flanders Dunbar[2] has well said "the ability to make a personality whole is surely as wonderful as the healing of a running sore."

These two disciplines, medicine and religion, should also be working together for the elimination of slums in America, which are a constant breeding ground for poverty and sheer human misery.

For competent and most helpful secretarial services in the preparation of this book I am indebted to Mrs. Dale G. Campbell.

To my wife, Bessie Carruthers Bonnell, I am once again profoundly grateful for her reading of the entire manuscript and giving me many constructive suggestions.

Office of the President   JOHN SUTHERLAND BONNELL
New York Theological Seminary

---

[2] *Mind and Body: Psychosomatic Medicine* (New York: Random House, 1947), p. 95.

Contents

1

The Healing Shrine of Lourdes

WHILE DOING research in the Academy of Medicine, Fifth Avenue, New York, on the subject of healing, I came upon an excellent discussion of the relation between spiritual healing and medical science. It occurred to me that in preparation of this book, I should visit a locality where both these vital factors in healing could be seen in actual operation. Where could this be done more effectively than at the Shrine of Lourdes, France? Immediately I put this ancient town into an itinerary that would take me to Rome and a private audience with Pope Paul VI; the Holy Land, with special attention to Nazareth, Tiberius, Capernaum, and other centers of Jesus' ministry; to London and conferences with Harley Street physicians; to Paris and religious leaders interested in healing.

Throughout my ministry I had repeatedly heard stories of miracles performed at Lourdes. In earlier years I had viewed these tales with a high degree of skepticism. Latterly, however, I had listened to them with sympathetic attention and interest.

Having completed my appointments in Paris, I found that the schedule of planes flying from Paris to Lourdes-Ossun Airport would involve delays. Therefore I resolved to travel by "Wagons-Lits" both going and returning. After a comfortable night's journey on the train, I woke early, and so eager were my anticipations that further sleep was impossible. From the windows of the Wagons-Lits

I watched with interest the unfolding countryside—verdant, beautiful. Lourdes is situated in southwestern France and surrounded by mountains of the lower range of the Pyrenees. It has a year-round resident population of about 17,000 inhabitants, but in times of pilgrimage the little town is crowded with double and triple that number of people. It has 400 hotels of varying quality, with some 15,000 rooms available, and also a wide variety of camping grounds.

Since I had made no hotel reservation I was especially anxious about getting good accommodations. Accordingly I responded to a cabbie who loudly announced, *"Premier classe."* The Hotel Bethany proved to be excellent from every standpoint and quite near the site of the church and Shrine of Lourdes. My bedroom overlooked the swiftly flowing river, Gave de Pau, whose course is close beside the Massabielle Grotto on the river's left bank. At night I could hear the roar of the rushing water.

Immediately after breakfast I made my way to the large area occupied by the hospital, the baths, the churches, and the all-important Grotto. A Mass was well under way when I reached the Grotto—a most unimpressive–looking cave or gash in the huge rocks that tower above and around it. This is the identical spot where it is believed by the faithful that Bernadette Soubirous saw the Blessed Virgin and was given instructions and revelations. All over the rocky walls and in many large candelabra were lighted candles that cast their glow over the Grotto. Thousands of candles are consumed every day in this most holy center of the Shrine. I noticed that many of the peasants begged from the attendant, whose duty it was to replace the partially burned candles, one or more of the cast-offs. I am sure these were treasured as precious religious mementos.

After the Mass the congregation of approximately eight hundred to a thousand persons joined in singing the *Ave Maria*. Nine times in succession these words were repeated in Latin: "Hail Mary, full of Grace, the Lord is with thee. Blessed art thou among women and blessed is the fruit of thy womb, Jesus." This was followed by the *Gloria Patri*. Over and over again the refrain was repeated. The murmur of these phrases could be heard in the area of the Grotto and the baths at any time of the morning or afternoon or night. They were repeated endlessly, thousands of times. Indeed, it was almost impossible to find any part of the vast Shrine area where small or large groups were not engaged in singing the *Ave Maria*. My first impression, and the more lasting, of the Shrine of Lourdes, is the exaltation of the Virgin Mary.

A large statue of the Virgin stands in the center of the plaza facing the church. It is surrounded by an iron rail with receptacles in which bouquets can be placed. These flowers are sold to the pilgrims and at no time were there less than twenty-five or thirty fresh bouquets surrounding the statue of the Virgin. Also circling the statue and outside the iron railing were stone kneeling benches, and seldom were these unoccupied. Oftentimes as many as forty or fifty persons were kneeling there—mostly peasants from France, Italy, and Spain. As one walks around the grounds one becomes aware of a constant succession of prayers. People individually or in little groups are either praying, saying the "Hail Mary," or singing songs in praise of Mary. She reigns supreme at Lourdes. To her is given the credit for the powerful intercession that brings healing and blessing to multitudes. As one Catholic pilgrim said to me, "Who is more influential in appealing to a son than his mother? Mary can secure favors for those in need better than anyone else." One who has been brought up in the Reformation tradition is bound to have a strong feeling that our Lord has a very much smaller place in the thought of these pilgrims than does His mother. It is impossible for mere words to convey the strength and sincerity of the universal devotion offered to Mary at Lourdes. It seems to be in the very atmosphere one breathes.

At the close of the Mass which was celebrated at the Grotto on the morning of my first visit, the "Hail Marys" and songs of praise continued unabated and always it was nine "Hail Marys" followed by the *Gloria Patri*. As I walked about the grounds I found myself repeating the Latin phrases until I was able to do a fairly creditable job of intoning the entire ritual.

From the Grotto I went to the baths. One reaches the bath-houses by walking along the Domaine[1] to the right side of the churches and past the Grotto. The baths are under one long roof and on the individual fronts of the different compartments are gables. As the people, men and women alike, enter their own individual compartments, the nurses and stretcher-bearers, and sometimes friends, help the patient to undress. If patients are able to walk, they go down several steps into the water. If they are completely helpless, they are lowered into the baths on stretchers or in the arms of attendants. It is deeply touching to see the relatives on the outside of the bathhouses, clustered together praying fervently. Sometimes priests from the country areas may be seen in groups or individually on their knees imploring the Blessed Virgin for a miracle of healing.

Most touching of all to me was a long line of little children. Some of these were less than twelve months old. Almost every conceivable illness of childhood was represented in that pitiful procession. Tuberculosis victims were there, thin and wasted; asthmatic sufferers, gasping for breath; epileptics—one had a seizure on his way to the baths; polio victims, many of them with iron braces on their bodies; spastics, turning and twisting—some flinging their arms and legs about. A pitiful little child, about fifteen months old, sat crouched in the carriage, his knees as large as an adult's closed fist, but his legs no thicker than a stout pencil. Mongolians were among their number and unmistakable idiots. Indeed, as the procession of sixty to eighty children passed, unless one were devoid of all feeling, unbidden tears sprang to the eyes and a feeling of great compassion gripped the heart. Looking at these little ones, one could understand why the manager of a hotel in Lourdes said, "The Lourdes Shrine is a place both of great faith and of great skepticism." The problem of human pain, illness, and suffering, especially in childhood, presents an incisive challenge to faith. One of the most touching sights was a boy about nine years old hopefully pushing a wheelchair in which his younger brother, aged five, was lying prostrate, completely paralyzed and blind.

[1] The spacious grounds.

At the Piscines, or baths, there is a special entrance for children. This is quite close to the one for the women. These entrances are nearest to the church. At the far end of the Piscines is the doorway for men. Six baths are provided for women and three for men. The proportion of women pilgrims to men is about five to one. A far larger number of women than men will be found in the list of authenticated miracles. Benches are provided outside the entrances. It was my good fortune, because of the early arrival of our train, to attend not only the Mass but to witness the coming of both the children and the adults to the baths. Most came in the three-wheeled carriages, pushed by faithful friends and relatives or by volunteer attendants. Those who were too weak to ride were carried on stretchers. I made a swift count of the women lined up, side by side, waiting their turn at the baths. At least ninety were present that morning and seats vacated were immediately filled by a constant stream of new arrivals.

Each day I was in Lourdes I watched this unbroken procession entering the baths. At times one has to turn one's face away from the horrible appearance to which sickness has brought these pilgrims. They are a study of almost infinite patience as with pale faces oftentimes distorted with pain, they wait hopefully and prayerfully for a healing.

A surprising number of them were sitting up in their carriages. Others leaned forward or backward in weakness with their burden of alternating fears and hopes. For several hours, until well toward noon, I watched these heart-breaking processions. It is said that some two thousands invalids can be bathed in four hours. This accounts for the fact that the line moved with little delay. What a mass of human suffering was revealed in this stream of men, women, and children coming to the healing waters! Patients with fractures and compound fractures of their limbs arrived in plaster casts and splints. Some were suffering from tuberculosis in its final stage; there were also the paralyzed; the twisted and tortured from crippling arthritis; the dropsied; some with horribly disfigured faces and others with constantly discharging wounds wrapped with dressings and bandages. One middle-aged man was so shaken with palsy that it was difficult to get him into the bath-house even with the aid of two devoted friends. The sight of all this human misery and wretchedness, this wreckage of human beings, reminds one of the passage in the fifth chapter of St. John's Gospel where we read: "Now there is in Jerusalem by the sheep gate a pool in Hebrew called 'Bethsaida' which has five porticoes. In these lay a multitude of invalids, blind, lame and paralyzed" (5:2, RSV).

The Lourdes pilgrims enter the appropriate doorway for each sex and find themselves in a vestibule where kind stretcher-bearers and skillful nurses prepare them for the baths. In each compartment there is a shallow stone bath with a few steps leading down to the water. Those who were unsteady on their feet were guided by the attendants and when they were undressed, around their loins was placed a towel that had been wrung out in the water.

Mrs. Ruth Cranston, who visited Lourdes, believed that, in preparation for the book she planned to write on the Shrine, she ought to submit to a bath in the Piscines. The moment before she descended into the icy cold water, she noted that the towel that was wrapped around her was the one that had been used on the preceding pilgrim.

In Lourdes, as elsewhere, one sometimes meets with strange distortions of the meaning of the word "faith." Dr. Weatherhead[2] points out that in the baths at Lourdes the outlet for the soiled water is high up in the large tubs—only a little lower than the intake. As a result the water changes very slowly and the contamination from discharging wounds remains a longer time than is desirable. He says that a priest told him that to prove his "faith" in the healing waters at the Picsines every time he took a bath there he cupped his hands and drank of the water.

Ruth Cranston[3] writing on the subject of the bath water says:

[2] Leslie D. Weatherhead, *Psychology, Religion and Healing* (Nashville: Abingdon Press, 1951), p. 147.
[3] *The Miracle of Lourdes* (New York: Popular Library, 1940), p. 39.

"The fact remains, as some writers have emphasized, that the water at the Lourdes baths is not changed after each patient. Some say it is not changed all day . . . Where two thousand patients are bathed in four hours, one follows swiftly upon the other. Persons suffering from syphilis, cancer, tuberculosis, and all manner of diseases, are immersed in the same bath water. The strange thing is that no infection ever results."

The testimony of the priest who drank the used bath water is more likely to produce in his hearers acute nausea than admiration. He should be reminded of the second of Jesus' temptations when he was urged by the devil to show his faith in God's protective care by leaping from the pinnacle of the temple. Our Lord replied, "Thou shalt not tempt the Lord thy God" (Matt. 3:7). It hardly need be said that the doctors at the Medical Bureau would highly disapprove the action of the priest, irrespective of whether or not infection might have resulted.

The procedure of the actual bath, when complete, meant being entirely submerged in the water for only a few moments. It is the custom not to dry the pilgrims off at the end of the bath, but to let them carry the magical water still on their bodies as they leave the Piscines.

While they are awaiting their turn and during the actual immersion, prayers are offered audibly by the pilgrims themselves, their friends and loved ones, and by the nurses and attendants so that there is a murmur of petition that never ceases.

Bathing at the Piscines was continuous from a period after the morning Mass until noon, and then resumed in the early afternoon until half past four o'clock when all of the sick were wheeled or carried on stretchers to the great ramps rising on both sides of the Basilica. Here they were gathered for an event of profound significance to every devout Catholic—the Procession of the Blessed Sacrament. Almost as many pilgrims are healed during or after the Procession as find deliverance in the baths. Indeed, on occasion the vast throngs of people gathered in the plaza have been electrified by the sight of some invalid leaping from his stretcher and walking in the Procession or even mounting the steps to the Basilica. To the credit of the authorities, ecclesiastical and medical, at Lourdes they discourage demonstrations of this type because they might readily lead to undesirable mass hysteria.

Before leaving the plaza in front of the Basilica in the early afternoon, I had neglected to look at the schedule of observances. Consequently, I was not aware that shortly after 4:30 P.M. the Procession would begin. When I presented myself at the lower entrance of the great Domaine, with the statue of the Virgin in the center, I found the gates firmly locked. An attendant informed me, however, that I could find my way into the enclosure by going up the side streets and entering by a gateway near the Basilica. Happily, I secured a standing place at the end of one of the ramps and had a splendid view of the whole proceedings. Later, I learned that the Procession had begun at the Grotto.

At its head was the Bishop with the Monstrance[4] under a brightly colored canopy. The Procession began its lengthy journey down the right-hand side of the plaza as one faced the Basilica and proceeded up the other. Leading the Procession was a group of some thirty schoolchildren—boys and girls with brightly colored banners and flags bearing the names of the Shrine of Lourdes and of their school. After this came another even larger mass of banners with the insignia of the various cities of Europe from which pilgrims had come. Following these were priests in their cassocks, some dressed in white, some in black, the bishops in purple and the archbishop in white and gold. One of the most colorful groups in the entire Procession was the nurses with their impeccably white uniforms and colorful capes. Finally, the doctors and the director of the Medical Bureau brought up the rear.

The singing was led by a quartet which stood near the entrance to the Basilica. Their voices were electrically magnified so that they gave magnificent leadership to the song of the multitude in the Procession. Thousands of persons among the spectators joined with the

---

[4] A vessel in which the consecrated Host is exposed.

thousands in the Procession in one great anthem of prayer, of praise, and of thanksgiving, with the song of St. Bernadette most frequently heard during the hour-long march. The chorus of the song rang out again and again:

Ave, Ave, Ave Maria,
Ave, Ave, Ave Maria.

During all this time, and for a considerable period before it, the sick had been lying on stretchers or seated in their little carriages on the semicircular ramps outside the church. The Blessed Sacrament was borne around the entire circle and, finally, a priest or bishop blessed the sick pilgrims, one by one, while thousands of others lifted up their voices in united prayers for a powerful intervention of the Blessed Virgin Mary. Even the most unsympathetic non-Catholic could scarcely remain unmoved in the midst of this exciting and vastly impressive spectacle.

When darkness falls, another Procession takes place, even more colorful than the one in the afternoon. The pilgrims purchase tallow candles or battery lighted ones. Those officially on sale are provided with a shade bearing the words of the Apostles' Creed. Even in photographs this Procession of thousands of lighted candles and torches is a magnificent sight. It resembles a veritable river of light. The climax of the spectacle is reached when the multitude kneels in the huge square and their voices ring out in repeated intercession for healing and blessing and peace.

Throughout the evenings the church is always brilliantly illuminated. From my hotel bedroom window I could look across the river and see the sky lighted as though by some gigantic fire. Making the situation still more impressive is the fact that dimly in the background tower the foothills of the Pyrenees Mountains. Quite unbidden come to mind the words of the Psalmist (Ps. 121), "I will lift up my eyes unto the hills; from whence shall my help come? My help cometh from the Lord."

In various parts of the Lourdes complex a most impressive prayer is frequently heard. Generally it is led by priests and may be spoken

in any one of a half-dozen languages: "Lord, we adore Thee; Lord,
we worship Thee; Lord, we love Thee. Lord, if Thou wilt Thou
canst make us whole. Lord, Thy will be done! Lord, we believe;
increase our faith!"

THE LOURDES WATERS

One of the most interesting features in all that Lourdes offers to
pilgrims is the Lourdes waters. Many of the greatest cures have
occurred at this point. The waters that now flow in such abundance
—they told me at the Medical Bureau that the flow is between
twenty-five and thirty thousand gallons a day—were quite unknown
before Bernadette discovered the springs. In the legend of Bernadette, it is said that during the sixth apparition of the Virgin Mary,
she said to the young girl, "Go drink at the fountain and wash
there." Following further instructions, Bernadette scratched away
the sand in a certain spot pointed out to her. First came only a few
drops, then a larger flow, then a still greater increase—and finally a
gushing torrent. Later, a turbine engine was installed to provide a
reserve to meet the demands of vast pilgrimages.

Very few people see the actual spring, which is behind the Grotto
on the left side of the altar. No one can reach it except those autho-
rized to do so, for there are iron bars over the openings and a pad-
lock. The water from the spring is piped down to the Piscines, or
baths. A long line of water-pipe stretches parallel to and resting on
the wall. At intervals of about fifty feet, taps are placed so that the
pilgrims, both sick and well, may drink of the water and allow it to
fall on their person, as was advocated in the vision of the young
French peasant.

Each day, morning and afternoon, I saw queues lined up at the
taps as men and women awaited their turn. They washed their faces
with the water, wet their hair, rubbed it over their necks and arms,
and the women on their breasts. In copious quantities they also
used the healing waters on their legs over their stockings. The men,
though much fewer in number, also eagerly applied the healing water
to their person. Most of the pilgrims carry with them a receptacle to

bear away some of the precious fluid. Every imaginable kind of utensil is employed. One of the most ingenious, which is seen quite frequently, is a plastic bottle made in the likeness of the Virgin Mary and equipped with a stopper. I noticed quite a few pilgrims filling these bottles. One man arrived with two glass flagons holding a couple of gallons apiece. He filled them full and went happily on his way, carrying one in each hand.

The Medical Bureau informed me that the water flowing from the spring has undergone every conceivable test and no healing agent, such as is often met with in famous watering places, is to be found in it. Therefore, the pilgrims say proudly that this fact establishes the grace and power of the Blessed Virgin. She, they declare, is the source of healing.

When one moves away from sights like these I have just described to hold conferences with the Roman Catholic physicians of the Medical Bureau, one becomes aware of a totally different intellectual atmosphere. I could readily sense that there are things going on at Lourdes which do not meet the approval of scientifically trained men. Yet, perhaps the majority of these physicians, especially the Roman Catholics at the Bureau, feel that there are popular forms of devotion that may have value for less sophisticated pilgrims. To the credit of the authorities at Lourdes, there is no sale of religious articles on the immediate grounds of the Shrine. The streets outside, however, are crowded with shops offering all manner of souvenirs, postcards, water bottles, rosaries, candles, images and notions. There are also wine shops and taverns.

THE MEDICAL BUREAU OF LOURDES

To me, one of the high points of my visit was several interviews with the Medical Director of Lourdes, Dr. A. Olivieri. He is not only director of the Medical Bureau, but also editor of the *Bulletin* of the International Medical Association of Lourdes.

I found Dr. Olivieri a most delightful person. He is somewhat self-conscious about his English and I had even better reason for similar feelings with respect to my French. However, using the two lan-

guages as best we could, I was able to get a reasonably clear understanding of the workings of the Medical Bureau. One soon learns
some rather astonishing things. Perhaps the most surprising of all
was to hear the director say that only sixty-two healings fully authenticated by the Medical Bureau and the International Medical
Committee are classified by the Roman Catholic Church as "miracles." From time to time I had heard passing reference to this fact,
but it is quite another matter to hear Dr. Olivieri saying it and to
receive from his hand a printed record of the sixty-two cures. This is
a surprisingly small result from well over a hundred years of operation. It must be remembered, however, as Dr. Olivieri was careful to
point out, that there are, without doubt, a considerable number of
persons in addition to the sixty-two who have been truly healed at
Lourdes, but for whom there are no adequate X rays, hospital
charts, and clinical records of medical examinations, so that they
cannot be classified with the medically verified cases. The Bureau is
at great pains to maintain accurate records. Yet even if one accepts
the more liberal estimate, made by some Church authorities, of cures,
this still would be a pitifully small number when one remembers the
millions of pilgrims who have visited this Shrine. It must be remembered, of course, that relatives of the sick and many additional people out of a fervent desire for spiritual uplift come to Lourdes and
are inspired and spiritually benefited.

Dr. Flanders Dunbar of the Columbia Presbyterian Medical Center, New York, says that when she visited Lourdes in 1937—and she
was deeply impressed by what she saw—17,000 people had come
seeking a cure. In 1954 the official statistics of Lourdes reveal that
the number had increased to 33,276. The Medical Director told me
that each successive year there has been a steady growth in the
number of sick persons arriving, and that in 1963, 45,000 sought a
cure.

He explained that the Medical Bureau urges upon all doctors who
visit Lourdes, irrespective of their faith or even if they have no faith
at all, to register immediately on arrival so that they can be con-
tacted when a meeting of the Bureau is planned. It will then be the

privilege of these doctors, quite a few of whom will be other than Roman Catholic, to come to a meeting of the Bureau when a prospective cure will appear. The opinion of all the doctors is solicited and they are asked to record their individual diagnoses and state whether or not they think a healing has taken place.

A second medical committee must validate all healings. It is called the International Medical Committee of Lourdes. There are thirty members on this Committee—all of whom in contrast to the Medical Bureau at Lourdes, are Roman Catholics.

The second great surprise for me was a statement by the medical director that every year approximately 300,000 baths are taken in the Piscines—yet, on the average only forty persons of that great total make any claim whatsoever to being cured. Of these forty, of course, there would probably be only one who would be certified by the medical committees as a verified healing.

Not all the doctors who go to Lourdes, said Dr. Olivieri, are convinced that a "miracle" has occurred. In fact the physicians in the local Medical Bureau and the International Committee never employ the word "miracle" at all. They say simply that the healing is inexplicable[5] to medical science.

These are the steps taken in each case where a healing is believed to have occurred: The doctor in charge of the group of pilgrims to which this candidate belongs goes to the medical director and reports a possible cure. The director calls a meeting of the Medical Bureau within twenty-four hours and also notifies all visiting physicians. If a negative conclusion is reached after an exhaustive medical examination, the inquiry is dropped. If the findings are affirmative the pilgrim is instructed to return home under medical supervision and come back to Lourdes after twelve months for further examination. If the healing appears to be permanent and there has been no evidence of any regression, then the pilgrim must appear before the International Committee of thirty notable medical specialists drawn

[5] "Incapable of being explained, interpreted or accounted for" (Webster's Dictionary).

from a dozen countries of the world. This regimen of repeated medical investigation must be continued for at least four years. In the case of the last two "miracles" proclaimed by the Church, the process took six years.

The final stage is the "Canonical Commission" named by the bishop who presides in the diocese of the pilgrim whose case is under study. Five persons as a rule are appointed to this Commission and at least two of them must be physicians. Generally these are international authorities in the field of the illness being investigated. When this Commission after prolonged examination substantiates the claim of a cure—*on medical grounds*— a "miracle" is proclaimed by the bishop or archbishop of the diocese. The following paragraph is the high point of the bishop's proclamation:

Having invoked the Holy Name of God, by virtue of the authority conferred on Us by the Council of Trent and subordinating Our decision to the Authority of the Sovereign Pontiff we judge and declare that the cure of————which took place on————is miraculous and must be attributed to the special intervention of the Blessed Virgin Mary, Mother of God.

Not a few Protestants refuse to accept the genuineness of healing wrought at Lourdes because the Roman Catholic Church attributes them to the Blessed Virgin Mary. There is, however, no such compulsion resting upon everyone who accepts these healings as authentic. A valid distinction may be made between the facts of the case and the inferences drawn from these facts.

The Medical Director of Lourdes himself makes this distinction. The conclusion that the Blessed Virgin Mary has performed the miracle is, says Dr. A. Olivieri, "an act of faith." However, freedom must be given, he adds, to another inference: "Freedom consists not in accepting or refusing to accept the existence of facts, since they are real, but in their *interpretation*." Even devout Roman Catholic doctors have their reservations. "Among Catholic doctors one finds sometimes the strongest conviction, sometimes the most stubborn skepticism. I talked with a number of Catholic doctors who were greatly interested in Lourdes cures but who are still uncertain as to the forces that produce them. . . . 'There are vast areas of knowledge as yet almost completely unexplored,' said one Catholic physician. 'All we can say now is that such healings are at present inexplicable.' "[6]

One of the reasons why only sixty-two cures have been officially recognized and recorded as inexplicable and miraculous may well be the rigid conditions laid down by Pope Benedict XIV as guidelines in the instance of what appears to be an unexplainable healing. Some of these requirements are as follows:

The malady must have been organic and not functional.

The healing must have been instantaneous not progressive.

The cure must have all the elements of permanency (durability). No case is authenticated unless four to six years of medical supervision have followed the cure.

A cure must not be claimed as inexplicable if any medication that could even partially account for it had been administered.

The cure must have been not only spontaneous but complete.

There must have been no regression in the patient's condition.

At this point it might be well to give a summary account of a typical "cure" which took place in recent years and which has been described with painstaking accuracy by Dr. A. Olivieri.[7] The proclamation of a miraculous healing in this case was made by the Archbishop of Marseilles on May 11, 1965. The medical director devotes approximately twenty closely printed pages to a discussion of the medical history of this one patient, Miss Juliette Tamburini of Marseilles. Understandably I shall be able to touch only the highlights of this report.

The medical history begins with the report of a qualified radiologist in 1952 when evidence was detected of the onset of a very serious illness. A collection of sixty X-ray plates was made across the years. No less than twelve separate medical files on Miss Tam-

[6] Quoted from Ruth Cranston, *op. cit.*, p. 90.
[7] The medical history of the patient in question is described in the *Bulletin*, No. 131-32, International Medical Association of Lourdes.

burini are available for the inspection of doctors with the report of exhaustive haematological, histological, and surgical findings. Here in brief is the medical history:

"For 11 years (1948 to 1959) Miss Tamburini suffered from a chronic, relapsing fistula (abnormal passage in an abscess) in the left thigh which ran a very classical course of periods of discharge, periods of pus retention, and acute exascerbations. During these eleven years Miss Tamburini underwent eleven surgical interventions (incisions and curettage of bone.) In addition she suffered from recurrent epistaxes for eight years which defied all therapeutic measures."

When Miss Tamburini, who joined a Marseilles pilgrimage to Lourdes in 1959, was taken to the baths she was too weak to enter the water of her own accord. Attendants immersed her in the water while she lay on her stretcher. On the evening of the second visit to the Piscines her physician was astonished to find that the wound which had been copiously discharging pus had suddenly and completely closed. From that day forward she suffered no relapse, and fifteen physicians who examined her at the Medical Bureau testified in writing of the completeness, instantaneousness, and durability of the healing. Each year she returned to Lourdes up to 1963 for further examination. The X ray revealed a normal bone structure and the disappearance of a former cavity. She received a medical certificate of healing for her osteitis. This young woman speedily returned to a state of flourishing health, going for long walks, riding a scooter, and following a strenuous program of night study.

Here is how Dr. A. Olivieri summarizes the history of this young woman:

1. On her arrival at Lourdes in July 1959 Miss Tamburini was suffering from a fistula in her left thigh. This was consequent upon a chronic osteitis of the femur which had persisted for eleven years, defying all therapeutic measures.

2. The condition was abruptly arrested in its course although it had shown no sign previously of improving.

3. The cure took place instantaneously without the use of any treatment.

4. This instantaneous cure that required no period of convalescence must be ranked among the extraordinary cures that are medically inexplicable.

AN APPRAISAL OF LOURDES

The first and most important issue that must be settled in the mind of informed visitors to Lourdes is this: Are these alleged cures factual? Did they actually happen as the Medical Bureau and the religious authorities claim? For me this question is no longer debatable. I believe that the sixty-two accredited healings, and probably many more undocumented cures, are authentic beyond the shadow of a doubt. The medical evidence is unchallengable.

One can readily investigate the credentials of the doctors who compose the membership of the Medical Bureau at Lourdes, and as well those of the visiting medical men who meet with them. This has been done in not a few instances. Not once has any evidence or even suspicion of fraud been found.

Similarly the thirty surgeons, physicians, pediatrists, and specialists who make up the International Medical Committee are all known to be reputable medical scientists and their names and addresses are regularly published by the Medical Bureau at Lourdes. Some of them are internationally noted in their fields. To conceive of these medical scientists becoming party to a fraud or even to a slipshod diagnosis is quite unthinkable. While at Lourdes it was my privilege to meet personally with several of these doctors and I was deeply impressed with the solid realism which governed their decisions and the manner in which they questioned the possibility of their own religious bias in their conclusions.

One of their number, who must go unidentified, said to me: "You should realize that all of us on this Committee are under subtle pressure—the pressure of the throngs that come to Lourdes annually —composed of people both sick and well—who are hoping and fervently praying for a miracle. The Church to which we belong would rejoice greatly in an additional manifestation of Divine power. But beyond all this there is the pressure within ourselves—as practicing and I hope sincere Catholics. We too would get tremendous satisfaction if we could produce incontrovertible evidence of a new healing that is inexplicable to medical science. However I can tell you with the uttermost sincerity that I have not known a single instance where these or similar pressures have carried any weight in our final decisions. Indeed at the present time we are scrutinizing all our procedures further to ensure that our conclusions are medically and morally beyond reproach."

An instance of the eager anticipation of the general public at Lourdes for word of a new miracle and the scientific detachment of the medical men will illustrate this point. One morning during my stay at the Bethany Hotel in Lourdes at the breakfast table I was approached by a friendly couple from California. Their faces were aglow with excitement. "Did you hear that another miracle has happened? A woman in the Irish pilgrimage who was blind has had her sight restored." On my way to the Domaine that morning several additional persons eagerly mentioned the possibility of a miracle. During the night the news had traveled swiftly throughout Lourdes. Arriving at the Medical Bureau I found the director talking with a well-known London physician who is a member of the International Medical Committee—Dr. Daniel O'Connell of Charing Cross Hospital, London. Dr. Olivieri was just remarking to his colleague that he planned to call a meeting of the Lourdes Medical Committee. This would include all physicians who happened to be on the grounds or in the city and who could be reached.

"Is there some special case you have in mind," Dr. O'Connell asked.

"Yes," replied Dr. Olivieri, "there's a woman in the Irish section who believes she has recovered her sight."

"Oh," said Dr. O'Connell, "I know that woman. She is rather neurotic. I think you will not find a notable improvement in her eyes."

"In any case," said Dr. Olivieri, "I am calling for a meeting at five o'clock today."

The medical director kindly invited me to attend with the doctors.

One or two skilled opthalmologists were present. There was undoubtedly an improvement in the woman's vision but this was a long way removed from a happening inexplicable to medical science or that could conceivably be classed as a miracle. Doubtless many people were disappointed that the hoped-for miracle did not materialize.

In addition one has only to read the reports written on individual cases of healing by some of the best-known medical practitioners in the United States to see how convincing is the evidence of authenticity. Among those are *Voyage to Lourdes* by Alexis Carrel.[8] The testimony of this internationally famous physician is the more compelling because he came to Lourdes full of skepticism regarding highly publicized cures. Describing himself as "a tolerant skeptic" he argues with medical colleagues at the Shrine Bureau, contending that the supposed "miraculous" healings were really due to the influence of auto- or hetero-suggestion, so powerfully present on the grounds of the famous Shrine. However, he would be willing to believe that some kind of miracle had occurred if he should see "an organic disease, a cancer disappearing, a bone regrown, a congenital dislocation vanishing." He then referred to a patient in the Sept Douleurs Hospital—Marie Bailly who was in the last stages of tuberculous peritonitis. The greatest shock in Dr. Carrel's life came when he saw this girl, whom he had repeatedly visited and given only a few days to live, suddenly brought back to life and health. A day or two before Dr. Carrel had noted the pallor of his patient's emaciated face, "her racing pulse—150 to the minute—the distended abdomen, her ears and nails turning blue." He told the nursing sister, "Her heart is giving out. Death is very near."[9]

A few hours later when his patient had been borne to the Grotto, despite his protests, he saw an extraordinary thing happen. After she had bathed in the Piscines, the appearance of her face gradually changed to the hue of health. The swollen abdomen was suddenly reduced; her erratic pulse became steady and normal, she was on the

---

[8] New York: Harper & Row, 1950.
[9] Quoted by Ruth Cranston, *op. cit.*, p. 143.

way to complete recovery. Dr. Carrel's complacency was wholly shattered, his smug philosophy swept away. Best of all, he has written a record of this and other remarkable happenings for the information of his medical colleagues around the world.

To this convincing testimony must be added that of my friend, Dr. Smiley Blanton of New York. At Lourdes and afterward he made an exhaustive study of the case of Charles McDonald of Ireland. Dr. Blanton led thirty-two doctors at the Medical Bureau of Lourdes in a study of this almost unbelievable case. Before a joint meeting of the American Psychoanalytic and Psychiatric associations, Dr. Blanton read an account of McDonald's remarkable healing. The facts were published in medical and popular journals across the United States and Europe. The medical certificate made out by a London physician stated that Charles McDonald was suffering from "Potts disease of the twelfth dorsal vertebra, acute nephritis, and tuberculous arthritis of the left shoulder." A sheaf of X rays and medical charts substantiated the diagnosis. Within four days of his being given a bath in the Piscines, rapid healing set in with complete recovery. Thirty-two doctors signed the medical report.

The third American medical practitioner who has reported on impressions received as a result of a personal visit to Lourdes is Dr. Flanders Dunbar.[10]

Among other matters Dr. Dunbar points out how a patient who is inclined to hysteria may mistakenly claim a miraculous healing. During her first week at Lourdes she saw two girls suffering from advanced stages of tuberculosis. After the bath at the Grotto one of them shouted, "I am cured! Our Lady has cured me." She became at once the center of interest and attention.

The other said quietly to her nurse, "I wonder if it can be true? I feel as if I were cured." She attracted but little notice. During the next few days the first had a definite regression and was being instructed by the Sister-in-charge on the subject of discipline of the

[10] See Flanders Dunbar, *Mind and Body: Psychosomatic Medicine* (New York: Random House, 1947), p. 93.

spirit. The second, for the first time in months freed from painful coughing and weakness, was now busy walking about serving her companions.

Dr. Dunbar was so impressed by the second case mentioned that three weeks later she visited the home of this pilgrim near Como, Italy, and talked with her physician. The small-town doctor was astonished beyond measure that his patient who, he thought, would not survive the journey had undergone a complete revolution in her condition and was now well on the road to recovery.

Facts, incontrovertible facts, cannot be gainsaid. They carry their own validation. And the healings that have taken place in Lourdes in the course of more than a century are established occurrences of this quality and caliber.

Now the interpretation of facts is quite a different matter and permits of far wider latitude than the recognition of them. The healing miracles of Lourdes are no exception. What is the significance of these remarkable happenings and how shall we interpret them?

For the devout Roman Catholic this will involve no problem at all. He has an answer, to him a satisfying answer, on the tip of his tongue. These miracles at Lourdes have come about, he will tell you, "by the special intervention of the Blessed Virgin Mary, Mother of God." His Church tells him this and that is quite enough for him.

But such a reply raises more questions than it answers. Not all Roman Catholic physicians will accept this explanation. I heard one of them remark at Lourdes: "The best one can say at this moment is that with the medical knowledge we now possess these healings are inexplicable." Even the Lady of Bernadette's vision gave no hint that *healings* would take place at this Shrine. She emphasized prayer and true penitence.

Mrs. Ruth Cranston whose book *The Miracle of Lourdes* has been highly praised by Roman Catholic prelates, in her first-hand account of happenings at Lourdes points out that religious faith and virtuous living on the part of the patient have little to do with a cure. She writes:

Devotion to the Catholic faith or to the Blessed Virgin apparently is not an essential factor. Some of the most extraordinary cures have happened to people of no religious faith whatsoever—such as Gargam, Auclair. . . . There is also the case of Germaine Birsten, a Protestant, in the last stages of Pott's disease. . . . A New England Congregational minister's wife, another Tuberculosis victim, had the same good fortune; and numbers of others.

If the question were raised with Roman Catholic Church authorities as to the specific role the "intervention" of the Blessed Virgin Mary involves, the answer would probably be made that she is a powerful intercessor. She prevails upon her son to perform the healing miracles. This, in my judgment, is not the belief held by the majority of pilgrims at Lourdes. I talked with a score of pilgrims on this point. Most of these were from the ranks of the less-sophisticated faithful, who make up by far the majority of those visiting the Shrine. Without hesitation they will say "Our Blessed Lady" performs these miracles. It is easy for persons untrained theologically to pass from Mary the intercessor to Mary the performer. Many illustrations of this transition will be found in books written about Lourdes. Generally the authors quote the exact words used by the pilgrims. One such author is Ruth Cranston. In her book already referred to, she tells the story of two children healed at Lourdes— one at the Shrine and the other on a pilgrimage train returning homeward. After describing the second healing Mrs. Cranston writes: "Everybody was in the corridor laughing and crying with the mother and *giving thanks to the Blessed Virgin who had wrought this double miracle.*"[11]

On the other hand, prominent medical men have implied that autosuggestion or hetero-suggestion due to the powerful impression of a multitude of prayers or hymns and mass enthusiasm expressed on their behalf was a prominent factor in these healings. Still others have put forward the idea that the infectious power of mass hysteria is the answer. Dr. Olivieri, Director of the Medical Bureau, has effectively answered these explanations by asking: "How could

[11] *Op. cit.*, p. 104.

suggestion or mass hysteria affect the thinking of those pilgrims who arrived in a state of unconsciousness or prostration or on the verge of a coma as Jeanne Fretel, Marie Mercedes and others, or children like Francis Pascal (aged 3½ years)?" Dr. Smiley Blanton of New York has made the interesting suggestion that in many of the cases of healing at Lourdes "there is a quickening of the healing process, due to the emotions aroused by the transference to an all-powerful, all-loving Virgin Mother."

All these ingenious and imaginative explanations of the mystery of Lourdes healings are but confessions of the simple fact that we lack any adequate explanation at all.

One fact seems apparent: the Creator has so fashioned our universe that there are inherent in it certain powerful forces that work for human restoration and healing. As man progressively understands the operation of these spiritual laws he will, under God, master the worst ills that afflict mankind. A thoughtful reading of the Gospel records of the life of our Lord reveals that he had deep insight into those spiritual laws that make for human health and well-being and that His life of perfect obedience to the will of God enabled Him to be a channel of the divine will and purpose.

It is much easier for us today who live in an age of nuclear power to accept the genuineness of the healing miracles of Lourdes than it was for an earlier generation. In the second chapter of this book we will note the testimony of front-rank scientists who tell us about the dematerialization of matter and the supremacy of the spiritual in the universe. With ever-widening knowledge of the universe and its laws breaking in upon mankind we shall, I believe, witness a tremendous forward step in the ministry of healing.

At the present time it is difficult for us to understand why one pilgrim should be chosen to receive the miracle of healing while thousands of others are passed over. Increased knowledge of God's ways of working in His world will bring deeper understanding of what at present is dark and mysterious. Truly we know only "in part" (I Cor. 13:9, av).

It will help to lessen our surprise and disappointment that so few

pilgrims at Lourdes find healing when we realize that physical healings, however miraculous they may be, are not the chief blessing
offered to pilgrims at the Shrine of Lourdes. Naturally a sudden
healing of a seemingly hopeless malady possesses a tremendously
dramatic quality which commands the attention of people everywhere. But these are so few and far between that this consideration
alone would never hold the allegiance of thousands of pilgrims who
return every year to Lourdes. They come for the spiritual uplift and
renewal of life which they unfailingly receive. Many come to care for
the sick and transport them to and from the baths. I talked with a
young Irishman who wore the harness of a *brancardier*, that is, one
of the sturdy helpers who carry the sick on stretchers. He said, "This
is the seventh Spring that I have come to spend my three weeks'
holiday at Lourdes."

"Isn't this a rather odd way to enjoy a holiday—moving constantly among desperately sick people?" I asked.

"Not at all," was his reply. "I am only one of scores of men and
women who do the same thing. I get such a spiritual lift in this
place—where everybody seems to be busy trying to help someone
else—and the whole place is throbbing with enthusiasm and good
will. I wouldn't miss it for the world!"

It would be a mistake to think that the people who are so busy
serving others belong only to the peasant or working class. Eminent
businessmen from various countries of Europe, teachers, professors,
lawyers, and clerks will be found among these helpers. Dr. Flanders
Dunbar of New York was astonished to discover among the nurses,
orderlies, and hospital aides in the Sept Douleurs Hospital at
Lourdes doing humble and even menial tasks not a few persons of
the higher ranks of European society and even one or two titled
women. A quiet spirit of self-dedication and self-giving permeates
the place. People do not appear to be depressed by the sickness that
surrounds them, for they move about the grounds in little groups
cheerfully and joyously performing simple tasks for others, singing,
praying, and happily conversing. A strong tide of spiritual enthusiasm sweeps through the throngs at Lourdes and creates an atmo-

sphere much akin to that of a powerful Protestant revival or an old-fashioned Methodist campmeeting. One of the doctors who is actively engaged on the International Medical Committee of Lourdes said in conversation with me: "It is unfortunate that so much of the publicity about Lourdes is concerned with the expectation of sensational healing miracles. Actually these healings when they occur are little more than fringe benefits. If Lourdes were a secular medical clinic and had produced only sixty-two authenticated healings in more than a century we should go out of business in a few months. The chief product of Lourdes is spiritual uplift and renewal."

Dr. Olivieri confirmed this viewpoint: "If you attend Mass and listen to the priests preaching to the sick you will find that they offer not so much suggestion of healing but sometimes actually countersuggestion. They urge the people to bear their sufferings in union with Christ and develop spiritual graces that will make them a blessing to others. Only incidentally do they mention the possibility of healing."

On my second day at Lourdes I listened to an eloquent sermon by an Irish monsignor. He addressed about one thousand English-speaking pilgrims. He talked about the spiritual benefits to be had at Lourdes, but only once did he mention God's gift of healing.

When it was announced in the American press that polio victim Fred Snite, the son of a multimillionaire, was going to Lourdes— iron lung and all—the news created a sensation. Would there be a notable miracle? Would this youth, who could breathe for only a few fleeting minutes out of the mechanical lung, return from Lourdes a well man? In response to questions from newsmen, Snite replied that the matter of a healing was in the hand of God. Of one thing he was sure—that he would return from the famous Shrine spiritually renewed.

This actually happened. The experience at the baths gave him a feeling of complete relaxation from inner tensions and an abiding peace. He returned to his home in the United States still paralyzed but with a far happier outlook on life. The final entry in his Lourdes diary says, in part: "Life here at Lourdes is so wonderful. . . .

Everyone is happy. . . . Here there is no talk of war, of politics, of [physical] bodies, here life is a prayer. It's no wonder we are happy."

For myself the one deep and abiding impression of my stay in Lourdes is the evidence met everywhere throughout the vast Domaine: *a universal desire to love and serve one another*. This spirit literally triumphed over the sickness and pain that was also present in such abundance. What other motivation is more sorely needed in our divided and loveless world?

2

Science and Healing

A PREREQUISITE to an understanding of spiritual healing is that we have an adequate philosophy of life and of the universe. Do we live in the kind of world in which it is reasonable to believe that healing may result in response to faith? Or, are we prisoners of an inflexible, closed, iron-bound system that permits no variations and is competely beyond the power of human thought and wishes to change? If the second interpretation of the universe be true, then it would be a waste of time even to discuss the question of spiritual healing. This viewpoint accords with the thinking of the ancients, especially of Greek philosophers and physicists. According to the earliest known theories of matter the entire universe is founded on building blocks known as atoms. These indivisible particles received their name through a combination of two Greek expressions—*a* (not) and *tomas* (divisible). They were regarded as final and irreducible. Of such particles, said the materialists, even the mind of man is composed. This materialistic interpretation of the universe and man held sway through the centuries among scientists and philosophers almost to the close of the nineteenth century. During the final quarter of the last century when such notable scientists as Darwin and Huxley entered the lists on behalf of materialism, despite the opposition of some eminent Christian men of science, it began to look as though the philosophy of the ancient Greeks must win the day.

At this time a number of writers appeared who began to use a popularized form of science to combat Christian beliefs and teachings. The name of one of these was Ernst Heinrich Haeckel (1834-1919). He wrote widely on scientific subjects, especially in the realm of biology. When one of his most popular books, *The Riddle of the Universe*, appeared in an English translation in 1900, it created something of a sensation. It was seized upon by skeptics and rationalists as a weapon that would put the forces of organized Christianity to rout. Haeckel denied immortality of the soul, freedom of will, and the existence of a personal God. Always he assumed that he was truly interpreting the inescapable conclusions of science. For a time his writings carried considerable weight in Britain. Yet the final verdict of history is that he can be given no serious place in either philosophy or science, as it has been definitely established that in bolstering his position he was addicted to a somewhat unscrupulous treatment of scientific facts. In the field of science especially, this is regarded as an unpardonable sin. No reputable scientist today would for a moment claim that the teaching of modern science is inimical to spiritual concepts.

It is not surprising that in the closing decades of the nineteenth century scientists in general, and physicists in particular, tended to become self-satisfied and somewhat smug. Dr. Robert A. Millikan, Nobel prize-winner of California, told a great audience in a Winnipeg church that European physicists by 1880 had come to believe that the millennium of materialism had arrived. An eminent German physicist with an international reputation, addressing a group of scientific students and professors, had said, "The great discoveries in physics have already been made. It only remains for us to perfect the formulations now known. . . ."

Said Dr. Millikan, as reported by the *New York Times:* "Within half a decade came Roentgen's discovery of the X ray. It was his photographs of the human skeleton that convinced even the sturdiest doubters. Swift on the heels of this development came the discovery by Becquerel in Paris of radioactivity: that mineral uranium emitted rays that penetrated solid objects very much as X rays do. That was in the year 1896, and it marked the greatest revolution in physics, up to that moment."

These happenings were followed, as we all know, by the discovery of radium by Marie and Pierre Curie and the earth-shaking (in more senses than one) event of the splitting of the atom in our time.

One highly significant result of these developments was the death-blow to the once widely accepted materialism that had largely prevailed from the time of the ancient Greeks. We are now witnessing the "dematerialization of matter."

Robert A. Millikan and Dr. Max Planck, perhaps more than any other of our present-century scientists, may be regarded as the apostles of the newer concept of the universe and of man. Early in the twenties in this century, Millikan drew up what might well be regarded as a scientific *confessio fidei*. During a period of intense controversy between some representatives of religion, on the one hand, and science, on the other, Dr. Millikan produced a statement that did much to reconcile the warring parties and to destroy what he called the "erroneous impression" that "science is materialistic and irreligious." This statement is reproduced here because the issues have probably never been more accurately stated. It was entitled "A Joint Statement upon the Relations of Science and Religion" and read as follows:

We, the undersigned, deeply regret that in recent controversies there has been a tendency to present science and religion as irreconcilable and antagonistic domains of thought, for in fact they meet distinct human needs and in the rounding out of human life they supplement rather than displace or oppose each other.

It is a sublime conception of God which is furnished by science, and one wholly consonant with the highest ideals of religion, when it represents Him as revealing Himself through countless ages in the development of the earth as an abode for man and in the age-long inbreathing of life into its constituent matter, culminating in man with his spiritual nature and all his Godlike powers.

This remarkable document, appearing early in this century, was signed by such scientists as Charles D. Walcott, geologist, president of the National Academy of Sciences, president of the American Association for the Advancement of Sciences, head of the Smithsonian Institution, etc.; Henry Fairfield Osborn, president of the American Museum of Natural History, New York; Edward Grant Conklin, head of the Department of Zoology, Princeton University; Michael I. Pupin, physicist and director of the Phoenix Research Laboratory, Columbia University; and eleven additional scientists including, of course, Robert A. Millikan. It was also signed by religious leaders.

Its publication signaled the beginning of a new chapter in the relations between religious and scientific leaders. If one notes the references to religion on the part of scientists from the twenties in our century to the present time, one is impressed by their recognition of spiritual values in the universe. Among these men are such notable representatives as Michael I. Pupin with his profound interest in the cohesive power of Christian love; Sir William Ramsey, president of the British Association for the Advancement of Science; J. Arthur Thomson, biologist and zoologist; James Rowland Angell, psychologist and president of Yale University; William Harvey Welch, pathologist, Johns Hopkins University, Baltimore; Arthur H. Compton, American physicist and researcher in nuclear energy; and Sir Arthur Stanley Eddington, British astronomer. These and many other Christian men of science of this earlier period unhesitatingly testified to their faith in the spiritual aspects of the universe. Not only so, but they effectively replied when their conclusions were challenged from within their own ranks or from beyond them. For instance, Sir Arthur Keith, Scottish anthropologist, when he was elected president of the British Association for the Advancement of Science in 1927, took advantage of the occasion to declare his disbelief in immortality. When the eminent British physicist, Sir William Henry Bragg, succeeded Keith to the same high office, he used his presidential address to affirm strongly *his* personal belief in immortality.

Perhaps we could choose no better representative of the period between the two world wars and shortly thereafter than the German physicist, Max Planck, originator and developer of the quantum theory which contributed so greatly to the development of physics and which won for him the Nobel prize. He has been called the "most revolutionary of all human thinkers."[1] In his *Philosophy of Physics* and chiefly in his *Scientific Autobiography*, Dr. Planck contended that science and religion constantly work together for the welfare of mankind. He expressed a deep appreciation for the stabilizing and healing powers of faith in God. In his *Autobiography* he writes:

And if we ascribe to God in addition to omnipotence and omniscience also the attributes of goodness and love, recourse to Him produces an increased feeling of safety and happiness in the human being thirsting for solace. Against this conception not even the slightest objection can be raised from the point of view of natural science. . . .[2]

In the last paragraph of his *Autobiography* Max Planck suggests that science and religion are partners in a common crusade against all enemies of human welfare and progress, and that their slogan must ever be "On to God."

The chief significance of this cooperative and friendly attitude of modern scientists toward religion is their evident recognition that the old materialism is as dead as an Egyptian mummy and that a new and more enlightened spirit between these two great disciplines now prevails. All that we have been saying on this theme was dramatically emphasized in a series of conferences by American philosophers and scientists at Wainwright House, Rye, New York, under the auspices of "The Laymen's Movement for a Christian World Order."

I was privileged to attend several of these conferences and participated in two of them. The conference which proved most fruitful was the one dealing with the subject matter of this chapter: the changes wrought in scientific thinking due to the new view of matter

---

[1] *Chambers Dictionary of Scientists* (New York: E. P. Dutton & Co., 1951), p. 362.
[2] *Scientific Autobiography* (New York: Philosophical Library, 1952).

and the disappearance of outmoded materialism. The comments of some of the present-day scientists who participated in the discussion are enlightening.[3]

Dr. Paul A. Moody of the Department of Zoology of the University of Vermont began by saying, "I like to identify myself with those who see in nature evidence of intelligent design, implying to my mind an intelligent Designer." Dr. Moody went on to suggest that "a similar faith is manifested by the physicist leading him to believe that the nucleus of the atom contains protons and neutrons because the nucleus behaves as if this were true." Then the professor adds significantly, "Similarly, if you go on the assumption that there is a spiritual design in the universe of which man's spirit is a part, *that faith releases power in the human spirit*—a fact attested to by the lives of countless men and women" (italics added).

The italicized portion of the last sentence stresses exactly why we believe that there has been entrusted to Christians, with other great undertakings, a ministry of healing which is in fullest accord with the spirit of present-day science. We are convinced that faith in God releases creative and transforming power, one manifestation of which is the spiritual energy that renews and heals human beings.

Dr. Edmund W. Sinnott, speaking on the suggestive title, "The Biology of the Spirit" gave an informative address at the previously mentioned Conference at Wainwright House. Dr. Sinnott was recently dean of the Graduate School of Yale. He is a botanist and biologist. The eminent scientist began his address by re-emphasizing the position of the physicists that a totally new concept of matter now prevails and that the old-fashioned idea of its being solid or corpuscular no longer holds sway. He sees evidence of purpose in the behavior of all living things and, as a scientist, sums up his idea of man's place in the universe in these words: "There is a good biological basis for the self and even if you will for the 'soul.' "

---

[3] All quotations from the addresses made at these Wainwright House Conferences are here given by written permission of Robert M. Cox, Executive Director, The Laymen's Movement, Rye, New York.

During the latter part of the nineteenth century and the opening decades of the twentieth, the lingering remnants of a materialistic and mechanistic philosophy among scientists and physicians discouraged Christian people and especially pastors from exploring the possibilities of spiritual healing, and from endeavoring to renew this ministry which occupied such a notable place in the life and work of the Apostles of Christ. If man is but a "physio-chemical mechanism" and nothing more, what purpose could possibly be served by a ministry of healing based on faith and prayer? It could have no valid place in such a deterministic and mechanized universe. Some of our most noted scientists have been among the first in the second half of the twentieth century to deny such a materialistic concept.

Dr. Wernher von Braun, who contributed so effectively to the United States missile program, is one of these. In his book *First Man to the Moon* he writes: "Toward the end of the nineteenth century most physicists had a materialistic outlook: they considered the universe as a kind of gigantic clockwork whose mechanism they thought they understood fairly well. The only role they gave the Creator was that he might have built and wound up the clockwork." He then notes the effect the discovery of atomic energy, the quantum theory, the splitting of the atom, and other such developments have had on the thinking of physicists and philosophers: "But the wonderful result was that contemporary physicists look upon the universe no longer as a gigantic clockwork, but rather as a great thought, a Divine Idea."

As one endeavors to document the history of biology and physics, especially in relation to the world of spirit, one is impressed by the complete change of climate during the last half century. The old belligerence and cocksureness of scientists of the nineteenth century has gone and in its stead is a deep sense of humility. As Robert A. Millikan stated it: "Science of the real sort is learning to walk humbly with God."

As the physicists study our universe by ever deeper penetration into the atom, the more spiritual does the cosmos appear to be. A professor of natural philosophy at Mt. Sloane Physics Laboratory,

Yale University, Dr. Henry E. Margineau, affirms that the old dog-matic physics of earlier times have been abandoned as hopelessly antiquated, that physical laws of the universe are themselves in flux, and that we must recognize as never before that "the Creator of the universe was indeed a mathematician."

Every additional discovery by the best accredited science of our time on this subject is further evidence that the universe is friendly to spiritual forces. One scientist[4] has suggested that it is conceivable that the entire material universe of which we are aware may one day be dissolved, leaving only nonmaterial reality.

> The cloud-capp'd towers, the gorgeous palaces,
> The solemn temples, the great globe itself,
> Yea, all which it inherit, shall dissolve
> And, like this insubstantial pageant faded,
> Leave not a rack behind.[5]

Is not St. Paul dealing with this identical issue when he writes: "We look not at the things which are seen, but at the things which are not seen: for the things which are seen are temporal; but the things which are not seen are eternal" (II Cor. 4:18).

If the new concept of matter as basically nonmaterial be true then the door to spiritual healing is flung wide open and its possibili-ties are boundless.

It is our conviction that we are faced with no rigidly determined cause and effect in the laws of the universe but, rather, with an ever widening field for the operation of spiritual forces. The Spirit of God touches the spirit of man and his physical body becomes a vehicle for the operation of God's will and purposes.

It is heartening to those who are working in the realm of religion, and specifically in spiritual healing, to have some of our best-known scientists testify publicly, and in some instances to their own scien-tific fraternity, of their belief in spiritual reality. Speaking on the

---

[4] Dr. William G. Pollard, head of Oak Ridge Institute for Nuclear Studies.
[5] William Shakespeare, *The Tempest*, Act IV, Scene 1.

subject of the "dematerialization of matter" Dr. Kirtley Mathers, Harvard scientist, said that, in the present stage of our knowledge, most physicists would hesitate to offer to their fellows a definition of matter. It is equally difficult, said Dr. Mathers, to formulate a definition of spirit. Nevertheless, at a meeting of the Geological Society of America in the course of an address, he had no hesitation in speaking of his own spiritual aspirations and of that part of himself that he was prepared to label as his "soul." "Spirit" for him is as real as "body." Dr. Gardner B. Moment[6] accords with this view when he declared "science is itself a manifestation of the spiritual nature of man."

If, as not a few scientists are suggesting today, the present concept of matter approaches ever closer to that of spirit, and the universe is no longer regarded as an inflexible, iron-bound system of physical laws, then we may well believe that spiritual laws operate throughout the universe and may well be the greatest factor in the cosmos working for the benefit of mankind. Let it be remembered that spiritual laws operate where physical laws are powerless to intervene.

People talk about the universality of the law of gravitation. So far as physical science knows, there is no part of the vast cosmos where its operation on material bodies and particles is not felt. Yet it is true that while physics can plot out more accurately than ever before the complexities of the law of gravitation, yet gravity itself is still largely a mystery. Many of the finest minds in the field of science have sought to penetrate its secrets: Galileo, Newton, Laplace, Einstein, and more recently Birkhoff, and yet its inner significance still eludes them. And the law of gravitation itself is really not capable of universal application. While man's body is subject to its sway, his personality and spirit decidedly are not. The truth is that while the organic and inorganic world of matter is subject to its influence there are vast and most important areas where the physics laboratory, the test-tube, the scales have no function to fulfill. No physical laws of

[6] A fellow of the American Association for the Advancement of Science.

the universe can permeate or exercise control in the realm of human personality or the spirit of man. Tennyson voices a deep truth when he writes:

> ... Tho' world on world in myriad myriads roll
> Round us, each with different powers
> And other forms of life than ours,
> What know we greater than the soul?[7]

When the present-day astronomer sweeps the heavens with his telescope and studies the laws that govern planets, their satellites, solar systems and incalculably vast constellations, he knows that within himself there is that which is greater than all the physical universe that comes within his ken.

Man's superiority over nature and nature's laws is not revealed in any capacity to annul these laws but, rather, in his ability to harness them and make them the servants of his will.

As Dr. Fosdick once expressed it:

Natural causation may explain the straits of Gibraltar, but it cannot explain the Panama Canal. Personal cause alone can account for that.

> "A man went down to Panama
> Where many a man had died,
> . . . .
> A man stood up in Panama
> And the mountains stood aside."[8]

In such a world as science has pictured there is ample reason and scope for spiritual forces and laws. God is not less free than the structural engineer who draws up the blueprints of a bridge, a tunnel, or a canal and then proceeds to supervise its construction. We should think of God not as residing outside the universe but within it, expressing His will in its laws though never a prisoner of them. He is both immanent and transcendent.

[7] "Ode on the Death of Wellington."
[8] Harry Emerson Fosdick, *The Meaning of Prayer*, in *The Three Meanings* (New York: Association Press, 1942), p. 106.

For if He thunder by law, the thunder is yet His voice."[9]

One of the perils that we face when we speak of God's healing power manifested in the lives of men and women through the ministrations of His Church, is that we are liable to present a picture of God, in the ancient mode, as outside the universe and occasionally breaking into the natural order to perform some miraculous works. Today our concept is much closer to the teaching of our Lord—that God is not only above the universe but also within it, not limited by its laws. Indeed the laws of the universe are but the expression of His will.

Sometimes medical scientists who are definitely "on the side of the angels" nevertheless express their faith rather badly. Dr. Olivieri has written these words, which appeared in a recent *Bulletin* from Lourdes: "All the same there are serious, honest, competent doctors who do not believe in miracles. We know this and are grieved at it especially when they are Catholics who by that very fact ought to believe in the possibility of divine intervention in the world outside the laws of the universe. I have often wondered what can have caused such a state of mind."

We must remember, of course, that Dr. Olivieri is a medical man and not a theologian. Certainly also he is not a philosopher. Some of us who believe with heart and soul in the reality of healing through spiritual power cannot accept the phraseology of Dr. Olivieri. He speaks of the "divine intervention in the world outside the laws of the universe." One sees clinging to the mind of the physician the ancient concept of God referred to a moment ago, as presiding over the world order and occasionally erupting into it to work a miracle. We must resolutely think of God's work in the universe as operations conducted through and by laws which are expressions of His divine purpose and will. No longer should we think of divine healing as a miraculous interference with the process and drive of nature.

I have purposely dealt at length with the changed attitude of science toward the claims of religion because this is equally true of

---

[9] Alfred Tennyson, "The Higher Pantheism."

medical science. It is most important that scientists in all fields should know what Christian pastors believe their role to be in the sphere of spiritual healing. The Christian teaching on this subject, too, should be explicitly stated. It is especially important that medicine and the ministry should have the clearest possible understanding of each other's role. That there has been a remarkable rapprochement between the Christian ministry and medicine in our time should be evident to all. The intimate relationship that once existed between medicine and the ministry is now being restored. These helping professions in a very real sense are working toward the same end as is evidenced by the fact that the Greek word for "to save" means also "to heal." Both professions are seeking to make men whole. In the early centuries of our era the office of physician and priest often existed in the one person.

An ancient Scripture known as Ecclesiasticus, which has been recognized by the Greek and Roman churches as part of the canon of accepted books of the Bible and widely used also by the Lutherans, has a notable word to say about physicians. The passage reads: "Honor a physician according to thy need of him with the honors due unto him. For from the most High cometh healing. . . . The skill of the physician shall lift up his head; and in the sight of great men he shall be admired. . . . His works shall not be brought to an end."

The author of these words, who is known as the son of Sirach and who penned them some 2,100 years ago, in that early period believed that the physician is raised up by God for the divinely appointed task of healing. He declares that there are two principal channels by which the gift of healing comes to man: faith in God and the skill of the physician. The words "From the Most High Cometh Healing" are carved in letters of stone on the archway entrance to the Columbia Presbyterian Hospital in New York. So the twentieth century A.D. is linked with the first century B.C. in proclaiming that the one Source of all healing is the Lord, the giver of life, the Most High.

Well-instructed pastors no longer tell their people that disease and pain should be regarded as God's will and that our duty is submission to them. Following the example of Christ, the Great Physician, they now declare that our mental, physical, and spiritual well-being is God's will for us and that we are most obedient to Him when we battle against the ills and diseases that destroy man's health and wholeness. Here medicine and religion should unite their forces in a common warfare. Then physicians of the body and of the mind may discover for themselves what a former Archbishop of Canterbury told the British Medical Association: "that the spirit [of man] quickened by faith and strengthened by discipline, possesses like medicine and surgery, true and great powers of healing which, like them, are the gift of the Most High, from whom all healing comes."[10]

Lord Horder, physician to royalty and recognized as one of the greatest of all British practitioners of clinical medicine, whose biography was published in 1966, wrote as though supporting from the medical standpoint the words of the Archbishop of Canterbury:

It is clear that there is a very definite point of contact between medicine and religion. Not only is there no opposition between them but they can and should be made complimentary to each other in relation to both the bodily and spiritual portions of a man's life. For the whole of man and not merely a part of him is concerned—or may be—in medicine, whether this be preventive or curative.[11]

Lord Horder's statement that modern medicine must reckon with the spiritual part of man as well as the physical points the way to a still deeper truth: that the physician is as truly an agent of God as the pastor. The same laws of healing operate in each of these helping ministries and they are God's laws. This is true whether or not the physician or surgeon is a believer. God's laws are quite impartial in their operation. When on rare occasions I meet with a medical doctor who openly declares that so far as religion is concerned he is an

[10] *Fortnightly Review*, February, 1939.
[11] *Ibid.*

unbeliever, invariably I tell him that nevertheless he is still an agent of God. On numerous occasions the Scriptures declare that God uses persons ranging from common people to kings to work out his purposes in the world. When King Cyrus of Persia sent back to Jerusalem all those Jews in captivity in Babylon who wished to return, the prophet Isaiah declared that this pagan monarch was fulfilling the will of Jehovah. Isaiah (45:1,5) sent this message to the Persian monarch:

> Thus saith the Lord to his anointed to Cyrus: . . .
> "I girded thee though thou hast not known me."

So, too, many a physician, psychiatrist, and surgeon who have never acknowledged God are notwithstanding girded of Him and are using the divine laws that make for health and well-being as agents of the Most High. Nevertheless the physicians' success in dealing with the mental and physical ills of their patients will be greatly enhanced if they are themselves undergirded by a simple but meaningful faith in God. As a notable teacher in Harvard Medical School[12] once put it: "The believing physician can often bring into perfection a cure not otherwise attainable."

A general practitioner whom I have known for some years as an eminently successful family doctor telephoned me one morning and requested that, as a special favor, I visit one of his patients. The man was suffering from angina. "I have been treating this patient for more than a year" said the doctor, "with discouraging results. His heart ailment is not severe but at times, about once a month, he has a painful attack and has to quit work and go back to bed for a few days. I have a strong impression that he may have a moral problem that he needs to discuss with a pastor and so I am calling on you. I have seen more than once what a bad conscience can do to a man in blocking his recovery from illness."

No small part of this physician's success is due to his spiritual sensitivity. The telephone call was additional evidence that he had

---

[12] Dr. Henry Asbury Christian.

the capacity to sense a deeper need than for medication in a patient's life.

When I visited this heart patient he welcomed me warmly but hedged quickly in response to even the gentlest probing of his inner life. During my third visit I hinted that it would probably be the last unless he proved willing to "open up" and tell me about his inner tensions and problems. Sensing that an opportunity like my visit might not come to him again, his tight-lipped reserve broke down and a story of moral defeat and bitter regret poured out. He had felt for some years that his wife was cold and unresponsive toward him, and he used this judgment as an excuse for illicit relations with a cousin of his wife. Since he had always been a person with high moral standards, his conduct had set up a severe inner conflict which greatly aggravated his heart condition. His repentance was now genuine and complete. Not only did he pray for God's forgiveness, but concluded the prayer with devout thanksgiving for the divine pardon which he gratefully accepted. No good purpose could have been served by a further confession to his wife, as it would only have made still another person unhappy. He made remarkable progress both spiritually and physically in the weeks following this interview. There was no recurrence of the monthly heart attacks. Aided by the skillful attention of his doctor and with a newfound faith, the patient has been carrying on his daily activities with only a few restrictions. This type of cooperation between pastor and physician is what we must encourage and constantly expand.

Medical scientists frequently refer to a mysterious force in nature known as *vis medicatrix naturae* (strength is nature's doctor). This appears to hold a balance in nature and seems to be working constantly toward restoration and healing. It does not provide an infallible remedy for all ills, though its influence is seen in every form of healing. A similar phenomenon is seen in the forest where nature heals the wounds made on the trees. If, for instance, an iron collar is fitted around a tree, little by little nature covers the iron completely and incorporates it into the tree, preventing it from stopping the flow of life-giving sap. It works on any injury such as a huge chip taken out of a tree. Nature begins at once slowly healing the scar made in the bark.

Biologists frequently refer to the manner in which nature sometimes restores missing organs. Fishermen too are fully aware of this particular phenomenon. Oftentimes they find in their traps a lobster that has a seven-inch claw on one side of its body and a three-inch one on the other. It had probably lost a claw in a battle with one of its own species, and certainly was growing a new one.

Dr. Peter P. Chase, in *Your Wonderful Body*, writes that when a foreign substance, such as viruses, bacteria and their toxins, enters the human body, immediately nature begins to produce antibodies to combat these harmful invaders. This is *medicatrix naturae* at work. Says the author: "In the event of an injury in man the cells that have been harmed spill out a substance that stimulates the remaining ones." This substance is called "collagen" and is astonishingly effective. It yields a gelatin which makes the white fibers of connective tissues.

Dr. Chase continues, "Certain cells in the body respond to toxin-producing bacteria (antigen) by reproducing antibodies which act to defend the body of the patient." The process is quite remarkable as he describes it. One antibody (opsonin) affects bacteria in such a way that it is more easily picked up and destroyed by the white cells. Another antibody—antitoxin—neutralizes the poison of bacteria, and still a third immobilizes the bacteria cells and clumps them together so that the white cells can remove them.

At the present stage of our knowledge we have no accurate and definable information as to how spiritual forces operating in the human personality can affect this process of healing. That it does so affect the process is beyond dispute, as is testified to not only in Lourdes but also in scores of other centers of healing and places where the prayer of faith is wont to be made. There is no shadow of doubt that in many cases where spiritual therapy has been used, often in cooperation with medical science, these resident healing forces within the human body come more readily into operation.

Recently I visited Dr. E. M. Found, superintendent of the Provincial Sanatorium in Charlottetown, Prince Edward Island, Canada. Dr. Found is past president of the Tuberculosis Society of Canada. He is an accepted authority in his field. I asked him to let me see some X-ray plates showing how healing operates in the event of tuberculosis. He brought out a large plate and illuminated it. Pointing out foci of infection in the lungs, he explained how the bacilli invade pulmonary tissue. From there it may spread to adjacent glands or may enter the blood stream. He said that if the patient had that God-given thing called "resistance," the process is stopped initially by white blood corpuscles which fight the TB germs so that a capsule of fibrous tissue develops around the microscopic clumps of tubercle bacilli. As a result the person develops no symptoms. One could readily see on the X-ray plate rings of calcium that had fenced off the bacilli. Indeed many people leading normal lives are unaware of the number of these rings that may at that very moment be in their lungs simply because the bacilli has not been permitted to develop inside them. I asked him to show me a photographic plate of a patient who had not followed the stipulated routine or obeyed the laws of health. In such a case the healing process would have gone into reverse. He produced another picture and there, plain to see, were rings of calcium broken open. The bacilli had escaped to reinfect the patient. A menacing relapse had occurred. I asked the doctor what he regarded as the most important attitude for the patient to assume with respect to his illness. He replied, "The faith of the patient in his own physician and especially in a Higher Power that uses the natural forces of the human body for his recovery." Dr. Found is himself a striking example of another potent aid in illness—the faith of the physician.

Dr. Anton T. Boisen, famed pioneer in the practice of pastoral counseling, used to tell his students that confidence and faith should be the property of all good physicians. This sentiment is in full accord with the viewpoint of Dr. Henry Asbury Christian, quoted earlier in this chapter. He added that, to his knowledge, sometimes a physician who was less learned and skillful than his colleagues would yet get remarkable results because of the confidence he inspired and the faith that he encouraged in his patients. The attitude of the physician is always quickly communicated to the patient. There are those of course who will reply at once that very few physicians have a meaningful faith in God and that they regard religion for the most part as opposed to the postulates of medical science. Dr. Karl Menninger pours scorn on such assertions. He writes: "There is a common notion disseminated by novels and sentimental television stories, that doctors are cynical skeptics and that they regard faith and science as antithetical. This of course is ridiculous. . . ."[13] He goes on to add that while not all physicians are men of faith, many of them employ faith in God as a hypothesis by which they live and work.

If it be true that a strong faith quietly manifested by a physician can be an important factor in his work with patients, how much more is this true of all pastors who minister to the sick. If, in addition, the pastor has himself experienced the role that faith can play in a serious illness, he will possess an inner certitude that spiritual healing is a reality. Thereafter when he talks with a sick parishioner he conveys not only with his words but by his entire personality a sense of assurance that restores hope to the discouraged and hopeless.

In my own case I have known so little illness throughout the whole of my life that there has been only one occasion which I can recall when my faith was really put to proof. If befell me recently when I was conducting a preaching mission in California. Quite without warning I woke up one morning suffering from a severe attack of laryngitis. I could scarcely speak above a whisper. To make matters worse I was billed that day to address sixty-five top executives of the Los Angeles area at a luncheon in Pasadena. I had been told that this was one of the most important meetings of the entire mission. Immediately I used what medication I had at hand, but the condition grew progressively worse. It was frightening to try to speak and not be able to make an intelligible sound. It was humiliating too, be-

---

[13] *The Vital Balance* (New York: Viking Press, 1963), p. 365.

cause I was proud of my record of twenty-seven years of preaching in the Fifth Avenue Presbyterian Church, New York, without missing even one service because of illness.

When the host-pastor came to take me to the luncheon he suggested that probably the use of a microphone would help me overcome my unexpected disability. When I had taken my place at the head table I discovered to my consternation that the slightest attempt at speech produced a sharp and disabling stab of pain in the larnyx. Seldom in my life have I felt so utterly helpless.

The thought suddenly came to me: You have often told others that "faith moves mountains" and overcomes seemingly impossible barriers. Here's your chance to prove that this is true!

The words of the Book of Job (4:3-5) also flashed into my mind: "Behold, thou hast instructed many, and thou hast strengthened the weak hands. Thy words have upholden him that was falling and thou hast strengthened the feeble knees. But now it is come upon thee, and thou faintest; it touches thee, and thou art troubled."

My faith was being tested as never before. Since I had no appetite for the luncheon and could not converse with my partners at the table I was able to give my whole time to silent prayer. Little by little the conviction was borne in upon me that I must and could fulfill this speaking engagement. When the meal had been served the chairman asked me if I were prepared to go through with the address. I whispered, "I shall do my best." He explained the situation to all who were present and it was evident that I had a sympathetic and appreciative audience awaiting my remarks.

As I rose to speak a prayer of affirmation was in my heart. "I can do all things through Christ who strengtheneth me" (Phil. 4:13). Yet even at this moment my faith was mingled with fear. Like the father of the epileptic boy at the foot of the Mount of the Transfiguration I could say: "Lord I believe, help thou my unbelief" (Mark 9:24). When I made an effort to speak, to my amazement my voice came out perfectly clear though quite weak. However, the microphone carried my words with clarity to everyone at the luncheon and I suffered no pain. From time to time for months afterward I had encouraging reports of the good that had been accomplished at this meeting.

But my ordeal was not yet over. The infection in the larynx was still active. My host-pastor drove me directly to the clinic of a well-known throat specialist in Los Angeles where an appointment had already been made for me. I have before me now the results of his diagnosis: "The vocal chords swollen three times their normal size. Their condition: flaccid, pulpy, entirely off-color and hemorrhaging." He advised me not to attempt my next appointment, which was at 11 A.M. the following day. I explained that I was to address a meeting of the Presbytery of Los Angeles in Pasadena. There had been a sharp cleavage in the Presbytery between those who upheld the "social gospel" and those who stood for the "gospel to the individual." I had hoped to reconcile the factions. Consequently it was a most important assignment. Reluctantly the doctor gave his consent but pointed out that it normally required a minimum of thirty hours of time for the medication he was administering to have its full effect. I replied: "Well you are God's agent from the medical standpoint and your effort combines with what faith can accomplish —and will, I hope, enable me to do this important job."

The following morning when we arrived at the church for my speaking appointment I was told that 450 ministers and elders were present. In the meantime, following the previous day's luncheon, word had got around of my handicap and scores of people had been praying for me. As I mounted the steps into the pulpit a passage of Scripture came into my mind as vividly as if a voice had spoken the words: "My grace is sufficient for thee: for my strength is made perfect in weakness" (II Cor. 2:9). Instantly a surge of strength and confidence swept over me and I knew that I should be able to speak with complete freedom. Although from the standpoint of time it was far short of the specified thirty hours needed for full benefit from the medication, the healing process had proceeded so rapidly that every person in the congregation with normal hearing heard every word of my thirty-minute address.

This personal experience of healing has left an indelible impression on my mind and given to me a tremendous reinforcement of my own faith. It was one more demonstration, if a minor one, of what medical science and spiritual therapy working together can accomplish for the well-being of man.

One of the most encouraging developments of our time is the new rapprochement between clergy and physicians or, as it may be expressed another way, between medicine and religion. Far back in the twilight era of healing the offices of priest and physician were combined in one person. The first hospitals were temples dedicated to Aesculapius, the Greek god of medicine. Many patients visited these healing shrines to be treated by the priests.

Then through the centuries came a cleavage between religion and medicine. The physicians turned toward the early science of Greek medicine and the Christian clergy lost the faith which was such a powerful factor in the life of the early Church.

Now the two are coming together once again. Physicians who for a time were quite distrustful of pastors and their ministrations are now discovering that they may well be most useful allies. The trained pastor can sometimes bring help to a patient at the point where the physician's efforts were expended in vain. It is no longer unusual for a doctor to request a minister to visit one of his patients who is overborne by a powerful sense of guilt or in whose mind and heart the will to live is ebbing away. The pastor, on the other hand, no longer thinks of the physician's ministrations as on a somewhat lower plane than his own. Furthermore he does not refer to his ministry to the sick as "divine healing" in contrast with the physician's secular healing. He now recognizes that all healing is divine healing. The doctor too is God's agent.

As evidence of the new spirit of cooperation and good will, chaplains are now found in all larger hopsitals. These are thoroughly trained for their responsibilities and generally attend the staff meetings in the hospital so as to become conversant with hospital routine and be recognized members of the helping team.

In all up-to-date seminaries today students for the ministry or priesthood are being instructed in the basic principles of psychotherapy, so that physicians need not be apprehensive when these young pastors visit their patients in the hospital.

We should labor earnestly and prayerfully to hasten the day when the scientific skill of the physician will be combined with the spiritual insight of the pastor to bring to a world of guilt-ridden, fearful men and women that wholeness of body, mind, and spirit which the Creator has ever intended His children to enjoy.

3

The Use of Prayer in Healing

IT IS HELPFUL to study the manner in which scientists regard faith in God and in prayer. They have their own unique way of expressing themselves. Their views are presented in a different idiom from that used by laymen. Consequently, their approach is often enlightening. Quite naturally their thought is colored by scientific training. What is helpful for them might not always be helpful for those who do not think in scientific terms. Nevertheless, their observations can mean much to all thoughtful people.

Some significant comments on prayer have been made by a well-known scientist, Dr. W. F. G. Swann. Dr. Swann is director of the Bartol Research Foundation of the Franklin Institute of Swarthmore, Pennsylvania. He is also senior staff adviser of Manklin Institute of Laboratories. He writes:

Just as an electronic apparatus can, by feedback mechanism, when it has a desire for more power, trigger something that has more power, it is not unthinkable that this mechanism, which we call prayer, may be a real kind of physical reactor in the universe as a whole so that the expression of its desire puts us in unity with the forces of the universe to bring into play very much greater forces than we ourselves can operate.

When we remember that the limitless energies of the universe are at the disposal of God the Creator we can better understand why the

Scriptures assure us that "with God all things are possible." How vain and foolish of us then to seek to define the limits of what God can do in response to prayer, whether this be in the realm of healing or any other area. Throughout the whole of the Bible, in the Old Testament as well as the New, we hear much about the possibility of drawing upon tremendous spiritual power.

In the Old Testament this power is called *koach*. In the New Testament it is titled *dunamis*, from which our English words "dynamo," "dynamic" come. This power, we are told, will enable man to accomplish what would be quite impossible for him to achieve by his own limited resources. Indeed when one reads of the activities of the Apostles in the early Church one is impressed by the fact that they were all "power-filled" men. This power comes from God. He is its source. There are many scriptural references to it. Says the Chronicler, "God hath power to help" (II Chron. 24:8). Job tells his friends that God's power is limitless. After describing the mighty creative works of God, he says, "Lo these are but the outskirts of His ways. . . . But the thunder of His power who can understand?" (Job 26:14). The Psalmist (Ps. 62:11) says that "power belongeth unto God." And again he declares that God "giveth strength and power to His people." Usually, this gift of power is linked to prayer, as in the case of Isaiah: "They that wait upon the Lord shall renew their strength" (Isa. 40:31). A little earlier he says, "He giveth power to the faint" (40:29). "As for me" says the prophet Micah, "I am filled with power and with the spirit of the Lord" (3:8). A most important reference to available power is that which is quoted by St. Luke in his Gospel. He tells how the people had crowded out from all the villages of Galilee and Judea and that the Pharisees and teachers of the law were sitting by. Then he adds, "The power of the Lord was with him to heal" (5:7). Here we see this power of the Lord definitely connected with the ability to heal. Let it never be forgotten that incalculable spiritual power is made available to us through prayer. It is a mighty resource for all believers. In the case of prayer offered for healing, by individuals and groups, it is well that it should be constantly informed and reinforced by Holy Scripture. God's promises and man's petitions must find common ground. They belong together.

Medicine prescribed by an able physician can do much to keep a failing heart at work, but in an extremely serious situation oftentimes the will to live, undergirded by faith in the power of God, is the more potent factor. I recall such an incident in my New York parish. An officer of the Fifth Avenue Presbyterian Church had undergone a series of extensive operations and was completely worn out. His surgeon said that while the operations were successful so far as the physical illness was concerned, he feared that the patient did not have sufficient resistance to make a recovery. His will to live had been sapped by weakness. When I visited the patient in the Harkness Pavilion at the Presbyterian Medical Center he was on the verge of unconsciousness. Several times I repeated in a firm voice a verse from the New Testament. Later he told me: "I could see myself lying on the bed while the real me seemed to hover above my body ready to part company with it. But there was something that called me back." The thing that called him back, as he afterward recalled, was the words of Jesus: "Have faith in God." As he lingered in that mystic vale between life and death this message carrying the authority of the Word of God reached deep into his unconscious and strengthened the will to live. This man has continued to be a source of strength to less resolute lives.

Paul Tillich has a pertinent word to say on this general theme: "The strong usually have a strong conviction. Everybody needs a place to stand upon. Without a foundation no strength is possible." He adds: "Don't give up the faith that alone can make you ultimately strong because it gives you the ultimate ground on which to stand. [It] points to something which lies beyond doubt in the depth in which many beings and all being is rooted."[1]

When Christian people come together to pray for the sick, what a difference it would make to their outlook and expectations if they could but see what is the ground of their hope. The Bible and the

[1] *The Eternal Now* (New York: Charles Scribner's Sons, 1963), pp. 150-51.

highest Christian experience unite in affirming that in calling upon God for help we are drawing upon the power that holds the planets in their courses and sustains the boundless universe. The universe is on the side of those who have found a Helper and Friend in God. This realization, in recent years, has been to me personally a source of incalculable strength. Perhaps the opening prayer in a service for the sick should begin with words such as these: "Almighty God, who hast created the limitless universe and callest all the stars by name, upholding all things by the word of Thy power, and who in Jesus Christ hast revealed Thy love for Thy human children, come now to our aid."

A moving testimony to the effectiveness of prayer on human personality has been written by Dr. Anton T. Boisen. Few indeed have so impressed their personalities on the ministers of this nation as Dr. Boisen. Not a little of his influence came from the fact that he himself had passed through the dark valley of mental illness and in its depths had found a deeper grasp of spiritual reality. He always believed that his final cure came because of the resources of the Christian faith. In an article in the Chicago Theological Seminary *Register* Dr. Boisen teaches a powerful lesson on the effectiveness of prayer, drawn from the experience of Jesus and His disciples in the Garden of Gethsemane. Following the arrest of the Master, the disciples one by one failed Him whereas our Lord went through the grim ordeal even to His death on Calvary with an unbroken spirit. The reason for the poise and serenity which Jesus showed in the hour of trial, he suggests, is found in the prayer three times repeated in Gethsemane. Jesus fought out the battle in advance and won it when the test came because He was prepared. The disciples, on the other hand, had slept through this period of preparation and as a consequence followed the line of least resistance when the hour of testing came. "In the case of Jesus," says Boisen, "prayer controlled His entire life." "Watch and pray" said our Lord "that ye enter not into temptation." He was fully aware that our ability to face a crisis is usually determined in advance. Prayer imparted strength sufficient to face any eventuality.

"Prayer," says Boisen, "may be regarded as a conscious attempt to bring our desires and purposes and loyalties to the level of the cosmic and make them something more than contemporary and local." Boisen considers that *belief in a personal God has a very great therapeutic value.* In prayer, man reaches out to a sense of fellowship with a Power beyond himself which he feels and knows to be real. It brings us into touch with Someone other than ourselves who is all-wise, all-powerful, all-loving, and who seeks only our good.

At some time in everyone's experience, however, there comes a period when one has met with disappointment in prayer. Jesus' prayer in Gethsemane was not granted so far as the cup of suffering was concerned. Perhaps at some time we set our heart on some objective and prayed earnestly for it and then received a negative answer. Such an experience does not mean that it is vain to expect an answer to prayer or that God will not or cannot hear our supplications. Rather, it may mean that we have confused and perverted notions of what prayer really is. Does the trouble lie with prayer itself, or is it due, rather, to our method of praying and the kind of things for which we pray?

Prayer, as we have already seen, is the greatest single reservoir of spiritual power available to man, yet it remains largely untapped, unemployed. Perhaps the best method of dealing with this complex issue is to clear away the tangle of underbrush that clutters our pathway. Let us begin by noting some of the things that true prayer is not.

First, it is not a blank check on which God's signature appears, guaranteeing us anything on which we may set our hearts. Infinite wisdom does not put itself at the mercy of the whims and foibles of finite men and women. Too often Christians quote a phrase of Jesus' contained in some promise that He has made and treat it as though it stood alone. For instance, they may say: "Our Lord promises anything that we ask of Him." Then they quote the words: "Ye shall ask what ye will and it shall be done unto you." But they have omitted the condition which precedes the promise: "*If ye abide in me and my words abide in you,* ye shall ask what ye will and it shall be done unto you" (John 15:7).

Second, prayer is not a "rabbit's foot" or other charm warranted to preserve us from misfortune. During the last war some such talisman was often carried by soldiers to bring them good luck. This is not an expression of faith. It is a reversion to primitive superstition.

Third, it is not a "parachute project" to be reserved for use in some extreme emergency. Dame Quickly in Shakespeare's play[2] says of the dying Falstaff: "Now, I, to comfort him, bid him a' should not think of God. I hoped there was no need to trouble himself with any such thoughts *yet.*"

In the 107th Psalm (vss. 27-28) we have a vivid account of a violent storm at sea. Also illustrated is a perverted notion of prayer which is still held by multitudes in our time: "They were at their wit's end. *Then* they cry unto the Lord." Prayer in such cases is reserved as a last resort in extremity.

Fourth, prayer is not just a special appeal devoted to securing "things"—not even such desirable objects as good health, good fortune, prosperity, etc. This type of prayer is too often given a central place in our thinking. While the saints and seers and mystics, who are experts in prayer, regard petition for material things as legitimate, they unfailingly relegate it to an inferior role.

Fifth, true prayer is never an attempt to change God's mind, or to bring Him around to our way of thinking. Infinite wisdom cannot be subjected to finite ignorance. Prayer is also not directed to overcoming the divine reluctance. It is not a campaign to persuade God to do something He otherwise would have left undone.

These five fallacious ways of looking at prayer are by no means exhaustive, but their removal will help clear the way for a constructive, true, Christian understanding of what prayer really is.

But enough of negatives. Let us now look at the positive side of

[2] *Henry IV*, Act II, Scene 3.

the picture. Is there a true science of prayer? We are using the word here in the sense in which Webster's *Dictionary* defines science: "Accumulated knowledge systematized and formulated with reference to the discovery of general truths."

Let me make a positive affirmation which I believe to be unfailingly true: *No true prayer ever goes unanswered.* But isn't this a contradiction of human experience? Don't we sing in one of our hymns: "Teach me the patience of unanswered prayer"?

It is quite true that a particular request which has been made in prayer may be denied, but true prayer itself never goes unheeded. Unfailingly, it brings a response from God. This divine response belongs to the very essence of prayer.

Why do we say that no true prayer ever goes unanswered? Because it is not a true prayer unless through it we confront God and have fellowship with Him. There is no gift of which the human imagination can conceive or that we can ask of God greater than this—that in prayer we meet Him and have converse with Him.

If Christian people could but realize this, if they could grasp this central truth, it would revolutionize their thinking on prayer. No longer would it be a drab, dull, pedestrian experience. It would begin to glow with unwonted radiance. Then how insignificant would seem those petty little concerns that we so often bring to God in the light of one, tremendous, overpowering fact: that in prayer we meet Him face to face.

You will probably recall an oft-quoted incident in the life of Phillips Brooks of Boston. A Harvard student sought an interview with him to get help with a personal problem. He spent an hour in the study of the great preacher. When he returned to his dormitory, a fellow student asked: "Oh, what did Dr. Brooks say about your problem?" "Do you know" responded the student "I forgot to mention it. It didn't seem to matter anyway after I talked with Dr. Brooks."

You see, the contagious power of a radiant and victorious personality lifted that boy far above his problem so that it didn't matter any longer. And what may not happen to you and me when we come into the presence of the Eternal God? That encounter with a Holy God can cleanse and strengthen, can exalt and redeem us, so that the problem that once loomed large, now no longer matters.

Augustine is at the heart of the matter when he prays: "Give me thine own self, without which, though thou shouldest give me all that ever thou hadst made, yet could not my desire be satisfied." Thomas à Kempis writes: "It is too small and unsatisfactory, whatsoever thou bestowest on me, apart from thyself." And George Matheson, the blind preacher and poet of Scotland, cried out: "It is Thee and not Thy gifts I crave." These men were all masters of prayer.

Dr. Russell L. Dicks, with whom I have often conferred on these questions, throughout his active ministry emphasized prayer and ministering to the sick. In an issue of *Pastoral Psychology*[3] he says that prayer offered during a visit to the sick should breathe a spirit of quietness and confidence. It should be spoken in low, clear tones: "In quietness and confidence shall be your strength" (Isa. 30:15). "Be still and know that I am God" (Ps. 46:10).

One of our most frequent failings in our ministry to the sick is that both Bible readings and prayers are overlong. Sick persons cannot sustain long periods of attention. They quickly weary, the mind goes blank and then the patient is disturbed with guilty feelings. The spirit of the prayer and phrasing of it are matters of great importance. The use of Scripture quotations which are likely to be familiar to the patient is also strongly advised. An instance of this would be such passages as "Rest in the Lord and wait patiently for Him" (Ps. 37:7). "The Eternal God is our refuge and underneath are the everlasting arms" (Deut. 33:27). Jesus said, "Come unto Me, all ye that labor and are heavy laden and I will give you rest" (Matt. 11:28). Silence may well be employed in such prayers, but the silence also should not be too prolonged else it too may become a hindrance and embarrassment to the patient. The use in bedside

[3] September, 1953.

prayer of symbols and imagery that suggest deep quiet and healing peace is always helpful. In the case of the patient who is markedly ill or weak it is reassuring if the pastor will hold the patient's hand while he prays.

Often in the bedside prayer there should be confession and the promise of God's forgiveness. Time and again I've seen evidence of a heavy burden lifted from the heart of a parishioner through the prayer of confession and the received forgiveness of God. After such an experience a seriously ill parishioner said to me, "Now I am completely at peace. My life is in the hands of God, whether it be for recovery or the end."

The prayer of forgiveness and of comfort might read something like this:

"O Spirit of Christ who in days of old didst pass through the multitude laying Thine hand upon the sick and the afflicted saying, 'Peace be unto you,' lay Thy hand now on this Thy servant and speak the word of healing peace.

"For the sake of Thy son who died to redeem us all, forgive this Thy servant all his transgressions and sins, and remove them from him as far as the east is from the west, so that with a heart at peace he may ever trust in Thy promises. We thank Thee O Lord for this unspeakable boon of Thy divine forgiveness.

"Above all else, may Thy servant feel Thy nearness around him and about him and may he know in truth that 'the eternal God is his refuge and underneath are the everlasting arms.' We ask it in the name of Him who is the Great Physician, and the Savior of men, even Jesus Christ our Lord."

RECEIVING THE PEACE OF GOD

While I was actively engaged in a pastoral ministry, I had a little two-page leaflet printed on the above subject. I made a practice of passing it out to patients whom I had visited, when I was leaving them, but first I would always go over the points in the leaflet. This is how it read:

One of the greatest obstacles to effective prayer is that we ask God for His spiritual gifts and then forget that we should go on to receive and accept these gifts. Jesus said, "Ask and ye shall receive" and added "Everyone that asketh receiveth." But that's exactly what we fail to do. We ask God for His peace and then assume our responsibility ends at that point. We are like the disciples who prayed that Peter might be released from prison. Then, when he was released they left him out in the street knocking in vain on the door. When the knocking became sufficiently loud to interrupt the little prayer meeting, the disciples instructed the serving maid to go to the door and see who was there. I can well imagine that the disciples then renewed their prayer, "O God be with Peter in his prison and if possible release him." The serving girl came rushing back to say that Peter was at the door. Instead of thanking God and letting Peter in, they suggested that she was mad to say such a thing. It might be his ghost or his angel, but it wasn't Peter. But Peter persisted in his knocking and finally they had sense enough to open the door and let in the answer to their prayer. They asked but they didn't go on to receive.

Our Lord has promised to us the gift of His peace in these words: "Peace I leave with you, my peace I give unto you: not as the world giveth, give I unto you. Let not your heart be troubled, neither let it be afraid." Now having asked for this gift we should go on to thank Him for it, accepting it by faith, and rejoicing in the possession of His peace.

Then follows a prayer of thanksgiving for inner peace. If the patient is alone this prayer will be, of course, in the first person:

O God who art the source of all peace, I thank Thee for this spiritual gift which I now receive and accept.

The peace of God is flooding my life.

The peace of God is coming into my life even as the tides come in at the flood, filling every creek and inlet with its cleansing waters.

The peace of God is mine.

The peace of God is within me.

Thou wilt keep me in perfect peace, for my mind is stayed on Thee.

The peace of God is now filling me with quietness, relaxation, healing, and inner peace.

I relinquish every anxiety and care and trust absolutely and wholly in God; through Him who is the Lord of Peace, even Jesus Christ. Amen.

Two widely separated concepts of prayer are held—the subjective and the objective. The first concept implies that nothing happens beyond the person who prays. The second suggests that prayer can accomplish things that may not happen apart from the fact of the prayer. The first concept will not be held by anyone who has experienced in his own life and also seen in the lives of others the power of effectual prayer.

The subjective results of prayer are not by any means to be despised. It inspires courage and kindles faith. It delivers us from uncertainty, instability, anxiety. It enables us to meet breast-forward the worst that can happen to us. But even with all this to its credit, prayer falls short of the highest Christian ideal unless it operates beyond the range of the purely subjective.

William James[4] declares that prayer in the widest sense "is the very soul and essence of religion." Without prayer God and man are left in mutual remoteness, "with no intimate commerce, no interior dialogue, no interchange, no action of God in man, no return of man to God."

James emphatically asserts that prayer means *"something is transacting."*[5] He adds: "Through prayer religion insists things which cannot be realized in any other manner come about: energy which but for prayer would be bound is by prayer set free and operates in some part, be it objective or subjecitve, of the world of facts."

That he does not confine prayer's operation to the subjective is clearly evident by a final sentence of especial interest to all who are concerned with spiritual healing: "As regards prayer for the sick, if any medical fact can be considered to stand firm it is that in certain environments prayer may contribute to recovery, and should be encouraged as a therapeutic measure."

While all this is true we must always remember that despite the power that is latent in prayer God's sovereign rule is never impaired. Above the realm of freedom and desires God exercises an un-

[4] *The Varieties of Religious Experience* (New York: Longmans, Green, 1953), pp. 264-65.
[5] Italics his.

abridged sovereignty. Consequently we must not pin our faith in God's reality on seeing some occasional manifestation of divine power rather than in His continuous governance of the world.

Prayer has a twofold effect: first on man, second on God. When we ask for God's forgiveness and God's healing, it is in the belief that His power will be released through prayer. We should keep ever before us in prayer the goal of the wholeness of the self, visualizing our personality as God-filled, and ask our petitions in the name of Christ Jesus who came to make men whole.

A famous French physician once said of doctors: "It is the physician's task to heal sometimes, to relieve often, to comfort always."[6] So should it be with pastors.

Dr. Sadler of Chicago in his book, *The Practice of Psychiatry* writes: "When we set ourselves to the work of collecting or re-collecting the scattered pieces of ourselves, we begin a task which if carried to its natural conclusion ultimately becomes prayer."

This notable psychiatrist of an earlier generation did a great work in training theological students in the art of counseling. In this quotation he stresses the fact that out of the experience of counseling in depth comes also a deepening realization of the need and the power of prayer.

Prayer releases energy that affects the material as well as the spiritual world. It has an impact on body, mind, and spirit. In the experience of prayer we seek Someone to whom the prayer is addressed and with whom we have contact; Someone from whom we confidently anticipate an answer; Someone who is not a prisoner of the laws of the universe which he has created; Someone who truly embodies the dynamic powers of the entire cosmos. Such a contact or communion or fellowship is, as already noted, far more important than any gift that can come to us, not excluding the gift of healing. In prayer we pass from man-centeredness to a God-centered experience.

Vida Scudder says: "God invites our cooperation in carrying out

[6] Ambroise Paré (1517-90).

His purposes. . . . Prayer is an energy as real as the energy that binds the planets to the sun."

It almost startles one to reflect that many lives which lack purpose and meaning would be completely transformed by a real experience of prayer. The heart-emptiness of multitudes in our time is appalling. Consequently, they have no inner strength or stability. They cannot meet the challenges of life. They go down in the conflict.

Charles Kingsley once wrote: "The comfort which poor human beings want in such a world as this is not the comfort of ease but the comfort of strength." How true also is Kingsley's statement in regard to the many who are on beds of sickness and pain.

When some three decades ago Dr. Alexis Carrel published his best-selling book, *Man the Unknown*, it created something of a sensation both in the literary world and in the realm of religion. When the book was published, Dr. Carrel was working in the laboratories of the Rockefeller Institute and concerning himself with experiments on the human heart. The book was more sensational because it came from the pen of an internationally known medical scientist. There is little doubt that twenty-five years ago no words from the pen of a scientist were quoted from Christian pulpits more frequently than these words from *Man the Unknown:* "Certain spiritual activities may cause anatomical as well as functional modifications of tissues and organs. These organic phenomena are observed in various circumstances, among them being the state of prayer." Somewhat less known was this paragraph: "Prayer should be understood not as a mere mechanical recitation of formulas but as a mystical elevation, an absorption of consciousness in the contemplation of a principle, both permeating and transcending our world."

The insights presented in the first quotation from Dr. Carrel are now commonplace in our time. But those in the second deserve further thought and exploration. Many people however are not aware that after the death of Dr. Carrel an unpublished manuscript was found among his belongings on the subject of prayer. Through the cooperation of his wife it was put into the hands of a Church of England clergyman in Surrey, England. In this manuscript Dr.

Carrel said, among other things, "A doctor who sees a patient give himself to prayer can indeed rejoice. The calm engendered by prayer is a powerful aid to healing. It is by prayer that man reaches to God and that God enters into him. Prayer appears indispensable to our highest development."

Over a period of a few years I corresponded with Dr. Carrel on the subject of prayer. The correspondence began when he wrote to me for a copy of an address I had given on this subject over a coast-to-coast radio network. It was evident from his letters that when he spoke of prayer it was not merely from a theoretical standpoint, but out of a long and fruitful experience in the actual practice of prayer.

Not only is all that Dr. Carrel says about personal benefits emphatically true, but there is an even wider benefit to prayer—its power to reach out and touch other lives. This inherent power of prayer is specially underlined in such expressions as "absent treatment through prayer." Time and again this was demonstrated in the ministry of our Lord. The power engendered by prayer reached out and touched the lives of persons far removed from him physically. This is the rationale of prayer groups in churches praying for people at a distance. That such prayers in these circumstances are effective is emphatically true.

One instance of such healing at a distance in the ministry of Jesus is recorded in the seventh chapter of Luke (7:1-10). The Greek physician tells us that a certain centurion's servant, who was dear unto him, was sick unto death. When he had heard of Jesus he sent the elders of the Jews urging him to come and heal his servant. They paid tribute to this Roman army officer, declaring that he was a very worthy man and that he loved the Jewish people and had built a synagogue in Capernaum for them. In the ruins of ancient Capernaum as they are today one can see the great blocks of carved stones that formed a Jewish synagogue. It was probably built a century later than the one constructed by the Roman officer. Jesus went with them, and as they neared the Centurion's home he sent some of his friends to Jesus saying that he wasn't worthy that the Lord should enter his house or that he should be allowed to greet him. "Just speak the word," he said, "and my servant shall be healed." We are told that Jesus was amazed at the message sent him by the Centurion, and turning to the people around him he said, "I have not found so great faith—no not in Israel." One might expect that so great a manifestation of faith would produce great results, and that's exactly what happened. When the friends of the Centurion returned to his house they found that the servant was cured. In this instance there had been no physical contact at all between Jesus and the sick man. It would seem as though humanity has been created in such wise that spiritual contact can be established between persons even at a distance. In a sense the whole human race is one.

Evelyn Underhill, well-known Christian mystic of Britain, has often spoken of the blessings that many people receive from prayer and the healings that are wrought through the power of prayer. In an article on this subject she wrote:

One human spirit can by its power and love, touch and change another human spirit. It can take a soul and lift it into the atmosphere of God. . . . Those in need of help will find that the praying person is a transmitter of the redeeming power of God. . . . The most real work that you can ever do should be that which you do secretly and alone. There is actually a mysterious interpenetration of all living souls. This is the secret of the communion of saints. We are not separate units.

This interpenetration of human souls has been demonstrated again and again in living experience. Every pastor who has truly employed the ministry of intercession can recall certain profound spiritual results that have come from group prayers. For a period of fifteen years in the Fifth Avenue Presbyterian Church of New York City, no less than ten prayer groups of persons of various ages and interests met weekly. From time to time reports reached me from these, intimating the power for good that had been exercised through their intercession. With one of these groups I had especially close relationship and from time to time had reason to rejoice at the results which followed from meetings devoted to special prayers on behalf of individuals.

Elsewhere in this book I've referred more than once to a confer-
ence on healing that was held in Wainwright House, Rye, New York.
Among those who were present on one occasion and gave addresses
were two of the best-known practitioners in the field of spiritual
healing. One was Dr. Albert E. Day, now retired from the Mt.
Vernon Methodist Church in Baltimore, and the other was Leslie
Weatherhead, who at that time was senior minister of the City
Temple, London, England.

Dr. Day emphasized the fact that we must be very careful of the
claims we make in the matter of healing. Always we ought to keep in
mind the minor role that we play in healing. We give these people
back to God in love and trust, and it is God who does the healing.
Dr. Day reported that in Baltimore doctors were sending patients to
him in increasing numbers because they were puzzled at times by the
problems of personality. They recognized that spiritual therapy can
sometimes bring results where medical efforts fail. Nevertheless so
many complex factors are at work in healing that the pastor must be
careful not to overstate the results.

Two major premises from which Dr. Day has always operated, he
told the conference, were these: First, God is immanent and
transcendent. He is everywhere. Yet God is greater than all else.
Man is potentially the instrument or agent of God. There is a sense
in which God limited himself when He made man sovereign with
freedom of will. Second, while God is mystery, there are clues to His
nature and purpose, especially as seen in Jesus Christ. God is concerned with health and wholeness.

In the course of his address to the conference, Dr. Day reported
that he could find nothing in Jesus' teaching that says sickness is
God's will. The fact that invalids have often become saints is no
argument in favor of illness. He believes that God wills health for
everyone. He has made us sovereign in our own lives and will not
transgress that sovereignty. The minister is only one part of the
healing team. God's agents in healing, said Dr. Day, are *materia
medica*, psychotherapy, surgery, and the prayer of faith. The work
that is done by physicians is not outside the sphere of Christ's King-

dom. He also made the interesting suggestion that one of the conditions of being healed is the willingness not to be healed. By this I am sure he means that God's will must be supreme in every situation, and to our prayer must be appended these words: "Thy will be done."

In line with what has been said about group intercession for healing of persons at a distance, we find much light shed on this theme by the Rev. Roger Squire of the First Methodist Church, Redbank, New Jersey. He gave an account of a very remarkable healing. This story was printed in more than one magazine.[7]

A parishioner, Bob Stout, was badly injured in a train wreck. Serious brain damage resulted. He was visited by his pastor, who offered prayer for the accident victim and his family. The patient's father-in-law telephoned to the church to say that he had called in a brain surgeon from Philadelphia. They were going to have a last-chance operation to see if the man's life could be saved. The minister assured the father-in-law that prayers would indeed be offered. On that very Sunday morning the pastor of the church went to the chancel early in the service and asked the whole congregation to concentrate on prayer for this man who was then going to the operating room. He suggested that they have a mental picture in their mind of Christ going into the hospital and laying his hands on Bob Stout and healing him. Shortly after the close of the service the telephone rang and Stout's wife, full of rejoicing, told the minister: "Something tremendous has happened. There is not going to be an operation. It was called off. At ten minutes past eleven A.M. my husband opened his eyes and began what the doctor says is a sure recovery." The pastor and members of the congregation are quite confident that the recovery began at the very moment when prayer was being offered by the whole congregation in the church at ten minutes past eleven. This was the moment when the service was interrupted by the minister to make his announcement calling the people to prayer. Stout's recovery has been complete. It appears that the railway involved in the

[7] Among them the *Reader's Digest*.

accident made a financial settlement with Stout. This he tithed to the church in recognition of the wondrous help that had been received.

The second renowned Christian healer to whom I referred a moment ago and who addressed the Wainwright Conference was Dr. Leslie Weatherhead. In the course of his address he related a happening in St. Bartholomew's Hospital in London. It paralleled the episode described earlier concerning Stout who was injured in a railroad accident.

Dr. Weatherhead's parishioner was suffering from a blood disease that offers great resistance to medical treatment. Indeed, little hope was held for his recovery. When Dr. Weatherhead visited the man he was so impressed by his parishioner's faith in recovery through the power of God that he resolved on a Sunday night to bring the case to the attention of his congregation at the evening service. The whole congregation joined in praying for the desperately ill patient in St. Bartholomew's Hospital. When Dr. Weatherhead returned to the hospital later, the nurse who had been on the case continuously said to him, "I've got good news for you. A strange thing happened. Last Sunday night around seven o'clock the patient showed signs of improvement. The blood that we sent to the laboratory showed that for the first time the patient had started making blood in his own arteries and veins. So convincing was this evident that we were able to stop the blood drip into his veins. This treatment had been given him continuously for many days."

Dr. Weatherhead told the conference that the most crucial problem facing the Christian ministry is to find relevant ways of cooperating with God. The universe is not a cosmos on the material level and a chaos on the spiritual level. It is cosmos all the way through. All is law. We have only begun to discover the vast resources of the universe's spiritual power.

Recently, when I had a conference with my friend Dr. Weatherhead on the subject of healing, he stated that in the clinic of his own church where psychiatrists and physicians work with him, the patient must be continuously well for at least a year before any claim of healing is made.

THE CONCEPT OF WHOLENESS

The prayer for healing is a prayer for wholeness. The word "whole" was often on Jesus' lips. It was his most frequent description of an act of healing. "They that be whole need not a physician." "Thy faith has made thee whole." "I made a man every whit whole."

Every illness whether physical or mental is a breakdown of wholeness. A recovery or cure means a restoration of this wholeness. The word "whole" is from the Anglo-Saxon word "hale." It means complete in all of its parts of elements. This emphasis underscores a point of major importance in the healing ministry of our Lord. He was not concerned just with some specific malady or fragmentary defect in sufferers who came to him. His healings were not an end in themselves apart from the major thrust of his mission. Rather, he sought always the redemption of the entire personality. He made it abundantly clear that the healing of diseases was not the chief objective of his ministry. Indeed, he deliberately moved out of certain communities because the crowds were determined to hold him constantly to the work of healing. His reply was "I must preach the Kingdom of God in other cities also, for therefore am I sent." He refused to be crowded into a single-emphasis ministry.

Our Lord combined preaching and healing, emphasizing the fact that they were but different facets of his mission. He never thought of any of these activities as isolated endeavors. When a disciple of John inquired concerning his ministry, our Lord replied "The blind receive their sight, the lame walk, the lepers are cleansed, the deaf hear, the dead are raised up, and the poor have the gospel preached to them." In effect, Jesus said healing and proclaiming of the gospel of the Kingdom belong together. As his own lifework began to draw to a close, our Lord commissioned his disciples in almost the same words as he used of his own ministry: "Preach the gospel, heal the sick." Consequently, the Apostles went forth fearlessly proclaiming the gospel, and at the same time manifesting the presence of divine power in their midst by healing the sick and the afflicted.

In the light of these facts it is difficult to see how spiritual healing

ever fell into disuse in the Christian Church. When in the past
churchmen were queried on this subject by members of the Church
who requested an explanation for the disappearance of a healing
ministry, the stock answer appears to have been: "In the early centuries of Christianity the task of the Church was so difficult and
fraught with such peril as to require a special manifestation of God's
power in the world."

It is worth noting that within the last ten years in Great Britain
two great churches established commissions to look into the questions of the healing ministry. The first was in England where the
Archbishop of Canterbury established a Commission on the
Church's Ministry of Healing in 1958.[8] This Commission preferred
the title, "The Church's Ministry of Healing" to "Spiritual Healing."
They felt that the first term was more descriptive. Said the Commission of the Church of England: "Jesus commanded his disciples to
preach, to teach, to heal, to bring to men wholeness and salvation.
They were commissioned to the healing of man in his physical,
mental, and spiritual life."

It would seem that the Church of England's findings through its
Commission were more realistic than the traditional explanations
had been. Postapostolic healings declined in the Christian Church
for two important reasons, they said: first, the general decline of
spirituality of the Church; second, increasing reliance on Greek
medicine.

In the same year the Church of Scotland established a Commission on Spiritual Healing. Its findings were very similar to those of
the Commission of the Church of England, including its explanation
of why healing has disappeared so largely from the Church's ministry. From a study of the Commission reports and our observation
of the actual facts, we are driven to conclude that the loss of interest
and of power to work miracles of healing has been due not to any
intentional design on God's part, but to the lack of dedication and

---

[8] Information is available at the Church Information Board, Church House,
Westminster, London.

faith on the part of his trusted followers. The Christ which the Church presented to the world through the centuries was as feeble a representation of the majestic personality pictured in the pages of the New Testament as are many of the modern portraits of Jesus compared with the radiant Christ in Raphael's paintings. Nevertheless, God did not leave himself without witnesses, and throughout nineteen centuries of Christian history periodically there have emerged a succession of personalities who have demonstrated what God can do in and through men and women whose lives had become channels of His power.

All true prayer involves not merely man's cultivation of his own character and personality, but it necessitates an outreach to God and a deliberate attempt to communicate with Him. This communication necessarily involves some hope of influencing God. There are critics of this aspect of prayer who would consider this whole idea of influencing God to be a totally unprovable hypothesis, and what is even worse, a gross superstition. Yet if there is any hope of our receiving the forgiveness of sin from God, this possibility entails the necessity of contacting and influencing the Heavenly Father because it implies confession to God, repentance and the receiving of forgiveness from Him. The Prodigal Son made a direct appeal to his father. He said, "I have sinned against Heaven and in thy sight and am no more worthy to be called thy son. Make me as one of thy hired servants." He confesses his total unworthiness and that he has lost the right to be called his father's son. He is no longer entitled to take a place in the family relationship. He will now be satisfied to play the role of the servant. Actually, what the son said was, "Make me one of your slaves." It was this plea for forgiveness accompanied by a confession of unworthiness and a spirit of humility that made it possible for the father to say, "This, my son, was dead and is alive again. He was lost and is found." I submit that this was a distinctly objective result of a young man's prayer. The attitude and the action and the spirit of the son influenced the father and made it possible for the father to do what he always wanted to do: to receive back and forgive his boy. It is never otherwise with God, as Jesus made it abundantly clear. The initiative was not all in the son's hand. Indeed the reconciliation of these two, and the redemption of the son was made possible by the forthgoing love of the father. Long before the boy returned home the father stood ready to forgive, but he could not forgive until the boy returned and demonstrated his willingness to become once again a member of the family and a true son of his father. It is expressly mentioned that the father ran to meet the son, fell on his neck, and kissed him before even a word of confession was uttered. But, of course, the boy's return in his rags and wretchedness was evidence in itself of a change of heart and of repentance.

But someone may say, "If God is good and loving and desires the best for His children, why should He not give the boon of forgiveness and health and prosperity to His children without their having to ask for it?" To come specifically to the subject that we are discussing throughout this book, in the case of a distressing and painful illness, why does not God cure it immediately and deliver His child from distress? The best answer I know to this question is that man's freedom is involved in the issue, and also what a theologian of an earlier century used to call "the perilous prerogative" of free will. Man is not an automaton upon whom countless and unrequested blessings are bestowed whether he wills it or not. According to the Scriptures, he is a child of God with the capacity to deny God's right to be sovereign in his life. He can rebel against the divine authority. This rebellion is stated in another situation in the second Psalm:

> The kings of the earth set themselves,
> and the rulers take counsel together,
> against the Lord and his anointed, saying,
> Let us burst their bonds asunder,
> and cast away their cords from us.   Psalm 2:2-3

In other words, let us deny his right to rule. This is oftentimes the attitude of human beings. God's love seeks to enfold and bless them, but they reject the divine approach, they refuse the divine offer, they rebel against the Lord and break His commandments. In prayer there is both a manward and a Godward outreach. In the Godward approach of prayer some things will not happen, indeed we may dare to say cannot happen in our kind of world unless this two-fold operation takes place: God's desire and intention and man's willingness to receive what God has to offer. This is as true of an act of healing as it is of the experience of forgiveness and redemption.

When we turn our thoughts to the world of medical research and practice, in this area too we see the part that must be played by both man and God. Here also someone may say, "If God is a good God why are there so many diseases in the world that remain incurable according to the verdict of medical science?" There is urgent need of finding remedies for a multitude of mankind's ills. Despite this desperate need, God does not write in the clouds the formula necessary for successfully combating and destroying diseases. In our kind of world man must struggle long and hard to find a remedy for the ills that bring such misery and suffering to the race. So we have a Pasteur discovering death-dealing micro-organisms; Lister in antiseptic surgery; Jenner with smallpox vaccine; Banting with the discovery of insulin; Alexander Fleming with penicillin; Salk with a conquering remedy for poliomyelitis, and scores of other noble souls who in hospital wards and in medical laboratories are "workers together with God" driving back the frontiers of disease and death. Every gain that man makes he makes through toil, struggle and suffering, and many grievous and bitter disappointments precede the final success. This is the basis on which our world is organized—a world of free men and women. Now, of course, there are some people today who believe that they're wise enough to be able to devise a better world than the one in which we live, in which all these blessings would come to us automatically. Yet, when one begins to contemplate the kind of human individual that would inhabit that world one shudders with horror at the thought that it might ever become a reality.

What is true of these medical discoveries in a measure is true of spiritual healing. It's not an escape; it's not a bridge built for retreat from life; it's not a safety first; it's not an avoidance of research and experimentation. Spiritual healing, too, calls for all that we have to give in self-sacrifice, in discipline, in long hours of meditation and prayer. Such healing is not accomplished through some magical incantation or muttering of certain phrases of prayers. It involves soul-searching and an earnest outreach of faith.

Among those who labor faithfully in this field, we think of the scores of dedicated men and women—hospital chaplains and devoted pastors—visiting in the homes of the people or going from bed to bed in the hospitals of the nation. Everyone who seeks loyally to follow the footsteps of the Master in this Christlike undertaking of healing must engage often in the ministry of intercession. Many people are unaware that the failure of a Christian to exercise this ministry is, in the pages of the Bible, labeled a sin: "God forbid that I should sin against the Lord in ceasing to pray for you" (I Sam. 12:23).

All of this is not to say that whatsoever we ask will unconditionally be given to us. Both implicitly and explicitly every reference to prayer in the Scriptures embodies the spirit of our Lord's prayer in Gethsemane: "Not my will but Thine be done." God knows best. His way will bring the largest measure of blessing to ourselves and to others. We can trust Him for the outcome. What God wills is always best. When His children pray for bread He will not give them a stone. Oftentimes when they pray for a stone He will give them bread.

4

Forgiveness, Hope, and Healing

IF ONE WISHES to develop a philosophy of healing, what better means can he employ than to study the healing ministry of our Lord. Let us therefore examine a distinctive act of healing performed by Jesus at the Pool of Bethesda. We may refresh our memory of this notable happening by reading from the fifth chapter of St. John's Gospel. The core of the story is contained in the first nine verses (RSV):

After this there was a feast of the Jews, and Jesus went up to Jerusalem.

Now there is in Jerusalem by the Sheep Gate a pool, in Hebrew called Beth-zatha, which has five porticoes. In these lay a multitude of invalids, blind, lame, paralyzed. One man was there, who had been ill for thirty-eight years. When Jesus saw him and knew that he had been lying there a long time, he said to him, "Do you want to be healed?" The sick man answered him, "Sir, I have no man to put me into the pool when the water is troubled, and while I am going another steps down before me." Jesus said to him, "Rise, take up your pallet, and walk." And at once the man was healed, and he took up his pallet and walked.

Attentive students of the Bible will note at once that in this version a brief paragraph has been omitted from the full text which appears in the King James rendering. The missing words are these: ". . . waiting for the moving of the water. For an angel went down at a certain season into the pool, and troubled the water: whosoever then first after the troubling of the water stepped in was made whole of whatsoever disease he had." The omitted portion is part of verse three in the King James Version and all of verse four. The reason for the omission of these words from the New English Bible and the Revised Standard Version is that they are missing from some ancient manuscripts and are thought to be a later insertion. There is practically unanimous agreement on the part of New Testament scholars that the suggestion of the waters "bubbling up," "being troubled," or "stirred up" is the explanation offered by a prescientific age of a mysterious phenomenon. Even the Rev. Dr. G. Campbell Morgan, a conservative teacher of the English Bible, declared that this was "purely a natural occurrence, an intermittent spring with medicinal qualities."

The science of archaeology has placed all Bible students deeply in its debt, and seldom is this more true than in the case of the excavated Pool of Bethesda. A thrill swept across the world of biblical scholarship when the news was announced of the discovery of the Dead Sea Scrolls. Not many people, however, are aware that when, several years later, the Copper Scroll was found and deciphered, it brought confirmation of the actual name and place of the Pool of Bethesda. The site of the pool was discovered in 1872 by Professor M. Clermont Ganneau. It was located only a short distance from the ancient Church of St. Anne. For over half a century the work of excavation has been going on intermittently, and the pool itself has been unearthed. Deep down in the excavation one can see today the ruins of a church built over the pool by the Crusaders. Visible also is evidence of the five arches or porticoes that had been there in the time of Christ. I had the thrilling experience of walking down the roughly hewn steps into the excavation to a point some sixty or more feet below the level of the street, where the pool is located. After visiting many of the sacred places around Jerusalem and realizing the uncertainty of the traditions that associated Jesus with these areas, it gives one a feeling of awe that here we know that the

Master walked among men and performed one of his great healing ministries.

Another interesting discovery has been made by archaeologists. Before the period when the Pool of Bethesda was used by the Hebrews, two shallower pools were employed by the disciples of Aesculapius. This discovery firmly establishes the fact that a healing shrine existed at this place for many centuries. Aesculapius was a Greek physician born in Prusa in Bithynia in the year 124 B.C. His healing methods were very popular in Rome near the end of the second century before Christ. It is said that he vigorously opposed some of the theories of the father of medicine, Hippocrates, and that he recommended such simple treatments as diet, bathing, and exercise. The temples erected to Aesculapius in Rome and various other parts of the empire were really the hospitals of that day. Schools of medicine embodying his teaching appeared in faraway places, including Jerusalem. Patients were encouraged to remain for a week or more at these healing shrines and it was believed that their dreams would assist in the work of healing when they slept in Aesculapian temples. Undoubtedly, therefore, the Pool of Bethesda had every right to be known as an ancient healing shrine. In one sense it was a public hospital and might even have been known as a "home for incurables." Here came or were carried the sick, the blind, the crippled, the palsied. It was a place of pain and sorrow, wretchedness and despair.

To Bethesda came Jesus also in the course of His ministry, and we are not surprised that He sought out the most hopeless invalid in a place where hope was rarely found. Moving quietly among the stretchers or mats upon which the sick lay, He came upon a man whose infirmity had lasted for thirty-eight years. Looking down at the invalid, with compassion in His eyes, our Lord asked him, "Do you want to be healed?" Surely the question was superfluous! If he didn't want to be healed why was he lying so long by the side of this pool? The question at first glance might even appear trifling, with an element of mockery in it. Why then did Jesus ask it? Undoubtedly it was asked in order to arouse the sick man's attention, to alert him to expect something to happen. A somewhat similar remark was made by Peter when he addressed the lame beggar by the Beautiful Gate of the temple. He said sharply to him, "Look on us," and instantly got the eager attention of the man.

But a second and more important reason doubtlessly lies behind the question asked by Jesus. He wished to kindle an expectant faith in the discouraged heart of this man. He was seeking to arouse his slumbering will to recovery. Without his inward consent, or at least some manifestation of faith, our Lord might well have been frustrated in His efforts to help him. The Gospel records make it quite plain that the absence of faith did at times impede His work. We read in Matthew's gospel, "He did not many mighty works there because of their unbelief."[1] It is possible that the lack of notable healing ministries in our own day may be due to a similar cause. Man's perilous gift of freedom of the will may, in a measure at least, block the purposes of the Eternal God, though the divine intention can never be finally frustrated.

Dr. Harvey G. Cox of Harvard, in a keynote address at the Church and Society Conference in Detroit in 1967, is reported to have said with respect to the future: "In Jesus Christ God has given it over to man. God has taken the mad risk of putting himself and his cosmos at man's disposal. He has identified himself unreservedly with the chancy experiment called man and the results are not yet in." Undoubtedly there is a measure of truth in these words, but the truth is stretched too far. It is not the death of God that is suggested in this assertion, but the abdication of God. It would be hard to believe that infinite intelligence would put itself at the mercy of the whims of finite man. An over-all providence or sovereignty is exercised by the Eternal God above human freedom and perhaps conditioning it.

Dr. J. B. Phillips' version of this episode by the Pool of Bethesda is graphic and enlightening: "When Jesus saw him lying there on his

[1] Matthew 13:58, recorded of our Lord's visit to Nazareth.

back—knowing that he had been like that for a long time, he said to him, 'Do you want to get well again?' "

Almost inevitably Byron's poem, "The Prisoner of Chillon" comes to our minds. The poet pictures the noble Bonnivard languishing in the dungeon, seeing his companions beside him dying one by one as the years and the decades pass by. Finally, a paralyzing inertia lays hold of him. His release comes too late to bring him any happiness. Byron makes him say:

> My very chains and I grew friends,
> So much a long communion tends
> To make us what we are: even I
> Regain'd my freedom with a sigh.

Yes, the prisoner comes at last to love his chains. The invalid, too, may love his couch. Most people engaged in a helping ministry can readily recall someone who took to his bed or couch for a lifetime on the basis of some paltry medical excuse. So Jesus asked the arresting question, "Do you want to be healed?" When the sick man was thoroughly alerted and his faith quickened, our Lord said to him in words that vibrated with authority and power, "Rise! take up your bed and walk." Reflect on the fact that nineteen hundred years after His life among men the spirit of Christ reaches across the centuries transforming the lives of men and women in our own time, and think what mighty compelling power must have been exercised when He laid His hand upon the head of a sufferer and said, "Rise! take up your bed and walk." In response to these challenging words this invalid of almost twoscore years, with one supreme effort rose to his feet, picked up the pallet on which he had been lying, and walked out of that desolate place.

If one were addressing a group meeting of Alcoholics Anonymous it would be unnecessary to explain the importance of these words: "Do you want to be healed?" These people who have battled through to self-discipline and self-control are keenly aware of the significance of the question. I recall some years ago asking Bill W., co-founder of A.A., "How would you deal with a man who kept

asserting: 'Don't worry about me, I can handle this myself'?" Bill
replied, "The most important question we ask any candidate is, 'Do
you really want sobriety?' 'Are you ready to stop drinking?' 'Do you
want to be in command of yourself and your situation?' " "And what
if he declines?" I asked him. "Well," said Bill, "we just have to let
him go in the hope that when John Barleycorn kindles a still hotter
fire under him, he'll be back to take the necessary steps."

No one has yet explored to the deepest level such potent factors in
recovery from illness as faith, expectation, and hope. No reputable
surgeon would dream of operating on a patient who had surrendered
to a "death obsession." It would be a losing fight.

The Chinese and North Korean communists, who are experts at
brainwashing, recognized the importance of destroying hope when
they worked on the American prisoners of war at the time of the
Korean conflict. They knew that if they could kill hope in the heart
of a prisoner they could have their way with him. The War Department at Washington a few years ago released studies that were made
of former prisoners of war who had been in the hands of the Chinese. It is evident as one reads their testimonies that the soldier who
lost hope was completely vulnerable to the enemy and could be
depended upon ultimately to do their bidding and speak the words
that they put into his mouth.

Dr. Harold G. Wolff, distinguished research scientist in psychosomatic medicine, cites the heavy death rate among six thousand
American prisoners of war captured by the North Koreans. About
one third of them died. It is often said that the main trouble with
these prisoners was that they were afflicted with "give-up-itis." It
came as a result of demoralization, humiliation, deep despair, and
deprivation of human support and affection. The prisoner became
apathetic and listless. He neither ate nor drank. He ceased to help
himself in any way but only stared into space and finally died.

In contrast to this, we are told that the Americans during World
War II lost 94,000 prisoners in Europe. These men were imprisoned
only about ten months. Less than 1 per cent died before liberation.
In the same war the contrast with the Pacific theater is painful.

About 25,000 Americans became prisoners of war. They remained imprisoned four times as long as those captured in Europe and suffered far more than they the effects of threats, abuse, humiliation. Their demoralization was often extreme. One third of these died before liberation.

Dr. Wolff adds:

In short, prolonged circumstances which are perceived as dangerous, as lonely, as hopeless, may drain a man of hope and of his health. But he is capable of enduring incredible burdens and taking cruel punishment when he has self-esteem, hope, purpose and belief in his fellows.[2]

The Rev. Dr. Ernest Gordon, Dean of the Chapel at Princeton University, in his book *Through the Valley of the Kwai*, himself a prisoner of war, says that as some of the long-time prisoners marched into the camp it was quite evident that they were marked for death. They lacked both faith and hope. As they trudged wearily along, he says, "Their faces were expressionless. The inner spark had been quenched. They had come here to die. Many had no recognizable disease that the doctors could treat in any way. They had lost their hold on life. They were waiting for death."

When faith and hope died within them there was nothing left to live for. How some of our men survived is revealed in their testimony. Here is what one soldier said: "The heat was on us prisoners day and night, and they never let up for a second. If we kept thinking how powerful they were and how weak we were we'd lose hope and end up saying 'What's the use. They'll have their way with us anyway.'" Then he added these significant words: "Without faith in God I should not have had the will to survive."

Dr. Karl Menninger has written on the subject of hope. Certain American physicians, among whom were Will and Karl Menninger, visited Buchenwald prison camp a few days after it had been taken by our armed forces. To their great surprise they found a group of physicians in this camp who had barely survived. The American physicians brought these prisoners together and gave them a dinner

---

[2] "What Hope Does for a Man," *Saturday Review*, January 5, 1967.

even though the "banquet" consisted only of army rations, tobacco, and wine. To these starving men it was a treat beyond description. The doctors told the story of their imprisonment:

These doctors, prisoners along with all the others, had followed the same routines of 4:00 A.M. rising, shivering roll calls, day-long drudgery on the Autobahn, shivering roll calls again, and finally a cold bowl of thin soup before they crawled up on wooden plank shelves to sleep. They were starved and beaten and overworked like all the others, with no reason to expect any other fate than miserable death and cremation which they observed about them daily.

Now comes the surprise. At night, when the other prisoners were asleep, these thin, hungry, weary doctors got up and huddled together in a group, and talked. They discussed cases. They organized a medical society. They prepared and presented papers. They treated sick fellow prisoners and made plans for improving health conditions. Then they began to smuggle in materials to make various medical instruments. And finally they built, of all things, an X-ray machine! The pieces had to be found somewhere; they had to be stolen, they had to be concealed in the prisoners' clothes; they had to be carried back to the prison on the long weary march after work. The guards had to be bribed or otherwise thrown off the scent. But little by little, with the aid of some engineers and electricians among the prisoners, these doctors put together a workable X-ray machine and used it, secretly, at night, in their efforts to ameliorate the lot of their fellow prisoners. This is what dedication to medicine and humanity could do—kept alive by hope.[3]

A side reference to the role of hope even in the lives of animals is quite notable. Professor Curt Richter[4] of Johns Hopkins University has reported experiments on rats. When the rats were placed in certain situations which permitted no chance for escape and left them no hope, even the most vigorous animals gave up the effort and rapidly died. After the elimination of the hopelessness feature, reported the professor, the rats do not die. The speed of their recovery is remarkable. A rat that would quite certainly have died in another minute or two becomes normally active and aggressive. Professor

[3] Dr. Karl A. Menninger, *The Vital Balance* (New York: The Viking Press, 1963) pp. 391-92.
[4] Report to American Psychological Association, September, 1956.

Richter says the chief and compelling reason for their death was the loss of hope.

Dr. Harold G. Wolff, quoted above, wrote in the *Saturday Review*, "Hope, like faith and a purpose in life, is medicinal. This is not merely a statement of belief, but a conclusion proved by meticulously controlled scientific experiment."

If a physician can write such words there are tenfold more reasons why a dedicated pastor could say the same thing. Even in situations not related to specific guilt and forgiveness, as in the case of the impotent man by the Pool of Bethesda, hope still works miracles. How many times has a pastor, standing at the bedside of a parishioner, seen the tides of life that were running out, dramatically turn about and come surging back when hope was born anew.

In a large Canadian city a woman seventy years of age was nearing death. She had suffered a severe attack of influenza. Just when most of her vital force had been spent in a battle for recovery, suddenly pneumonia set in. She was not able to speak above a whisper or to take any nourishment. Her family despaired of her life and the doctor on the case admitted there was nothing more that he could do. "After all, remember," he said, "she's threescore years and ten." Just when it appeared that the end of life was inevitable, word reached the family that the woman's former pastor whom she had known for many years, loved and trusted, had arrived in the city and was on his way to visit this family. He was a wise and thoroughly experienced man, so when the news of the aging mother's condition was explained to him, and especially the fact that she herself appeared to have given up hope, he went into action immediately. He sat at the bedside of his former parishioner and took her hand. She recognized him. He had seen her through many deep waters in earlier years, and now she was overjoyed to have him so near. She whispered to him, "I haven't got the strength any longer to hold on. My faith in God is weakening." His reply was, "You don't need to hold on. It's not your hold on God that counts. It is His grip on you. Just relax. You're resting on the Everlasting Arms. God is taking care of you. His strength, His power, is flowing into you. Your family still needs you. We all love you. We want you to stay with us, and God is helping you now to do just that." He had prayer with her—a prayer that lifted her into the divine presence. Within the space of an hour her condition began to improve. Light came back into her eyes and her voice appreciably strengthened. The tide had turned and she was now on the road to eventual recovery. Faith and hope, when they come to even the most hopeless, turn impending defeat into victory. In such an instance as I have described, even if there had been no turn to recovery, faith would have transformed the closing hours of life into a time of spiritual exaltation and radiant peace. Like Dwight L. Moody near the end of his life, she too would have been able to say, "There is no dark valley here." The advent of hope can be "drums and bugles" to the human spirit, a presage of coming victory.

The role of hope in human well-being is not by any means confined to those who have come a long way in life or who are desperately ill. It can be a day-by-day tonic and inspiration, and source of inner strength to the vigorous and youthful who are facing life's difficulties in business or professional careers. It will hold us steadfast in the hour of trial.

Turning our attention once more to the story of the healing by the Pool of Bethesda we find that there is another facet in it that could easily be overlooked. Naturally the conversation between Jesus and this crippled man by the poolside is greatly condensed and only a portion of it given. When Jesus healed this man he knew that the illness that had kept him by that poolside for thirty-eight years had been brought on by his own folly. After the healing Jesus met the man in the temple area and said, "Now that you are well again, leave your sinful ways, or you may suffer something worse." It was after this that he went away and told the religious authorities that it was Jesus who had cured him. When the religious authorities on another occasion had charged Jesus with breaking the Sabbath law, he replied, "You are objecting because I made a man every whit whole." It is clear that there was more than meets the eye in this act of healing by the pool. A deep spiritual renewal had taken place as well as physical restoration. Jesus had made this man whole.

Forgiveness and spiritual healing are closely linked together. A professor in the medical department of Johns Hopkins University, in an address at the Academy of Medicine, New York, a few years ago said, "Man is a unity of body, mind and spirit and medicine must be aware of this unity. Physiology, chemistry and biology cannot alone or together explain the intricacies of life. A disturbance in body, mind or spirit cannot be confined to one area or dealt with separately. There is a wholeness in man that is interdependent." This viewpoint is now universally accepted in medical science, as we shall see in the chapter on psychosomatic medicine.

In Great Britain, too, this subject has been very much to the fore. The British Medical Association has declared that there exists a field for legitimate and valuable cooperation between the clergy and doctors; that working together they can encourage a dynamic philosophy of health. The clergy on their part freely recognize the physician as an agent of God in the work of healing. As we study the healing ministry of our Lord, we cannot fail to note that the confession and forgiveness of sins appears in some instances to have a determinative role in His healing miracles. The healing of the soul is to be recognized as something even more important than the healing of the body. In some instances of our Lord's ministry these occur simultaneously. Whenever he said to those who came to him for healing, "Thy sins are forgiven thee, go in peace" we may be sure that the alienation from God within the life of the individual had first to be healed and his sins forgiven before he could receive the inner peace so sorely lacking.

In the light of all these considerations and without insulting our intelligence, it is perfectly possible for us to see how a helpless, hopeless man by the Pool of Bethesda could, in response to the challenge of the Great Physician, rise up in new-found strength, take up his bed, and go on his way rejoicing.

While we must make it abundantly clear that all illness is not due to sin, nevertheless, one of my deepest convictions and one that has strengthened across the years, is this: a therapeutic force of great value to mankind is the received forgiveness of God. This is due to the fact that one of the root causes of most of the emotional maladjustments and psychosomatic illnesses in our civilization is an unrelieved sense of guilt.

In the sixth century before Christ, so an ancient fable tells us, a well-loved Greek lyric poet, Ibycus,[5] met a tragic death. He was on his way to the musical competition at Corinth. En route he was attacked and killed by two robbers, but before he expired he called upon a flock of cranes flying overhead to avenge his death. All Greece was shocked and dismayed by the news of this terrible crime and the people urged the magistrates to discover and punish the criminals. It would seem, however, that only the all-discerning sun could identify the guilty, for it appeared that no other eye had beheld the crime.

A few days later in Corinth in a theater open to the sky, a huge audience sat spellbound listening to a group of choristers who impersonated the avenging Furies. In solemn step the singers slowly advanced, clad in black robes and carrying torches that blazed with a pitchy flame. Their cheeks were bloodless, and writhing serpents in place of hair crowned their brows. As their weird song telling of the certainty of vengeance rose higher and higher it paralyzed the hearts and chilled the blood of the hearers.

At this moment a flock of cranes swept across the sky, passing low over the theater. Instantly a cry of terror rose from the uppermost benches, "Look! Look! comrade, yonder are the cranes of Ibycus!" Instantly the people knew that the murderer had informed against himself. The two guilty men were seized, tried, condemned, and suffered the punishment they richly deserved.[6]

This ancient tale from the pen of Plutarch illustrates a truth that

[5] The story is retold in Schiller's beautiful ballad.
[6] From Thomas Bullfinch, *The Age of Fable* (New York: Henry Holt, n.d.), p. 227.

has been known to mankind since the dawn of civilization: the destructive power of a guilty conscience. The avenging Furies on the Corinthian stage were portraying outwardly, in the form of a tragic drama, what is essentially a fact of inner experience.

The experience of guilt is an elemental fact of human life. Guilt feelings and conflicts can hamper, torment, and cripple a personality. In not a few cases it has been known to produce organic illnesses. An unrelieved feeling of guilt has even driven people to suicide or madness. When once a sense of guilt becomes powerful, there is a strong need in the distressed individual for self-punishment. People punish themselves by contracting various forms of emotional and physical illnesses. Some medical texts dealing with psychosomatic medicine list a whole series of illnesses produced through self-punishment.

In his writings, Dr. Karl A. Menninger frequently refers to that powerful impulse in anxious and neurotic persons to have their daily stint of punishment and pain. He says, "We know that every man decrees and executes judgments and punishment upon himself."[7] Dr. Menninger cites the case of a man who is driven by a tyrannical conscience to attempt suicide under the pressure of the urge to punish himself for offenses that he had committed.

American newspapers carried an item some years ago about a well-known forger who, during his time in the penitentiary, was making a strenuous effort to reform. Shortly before his discharge he suffered a paralysis of the right hand and arm which made it impossible for him to write. There was no adequate explanation of this happening except that it was the method chosen by his unconscious self to make forgery on his part forever impossible. More than one psychiatrist has told of a patient who developed serious eye trouble as he battled his major temptation to become a "peeping Tom."

Dr. Alphonse Maeder, one of Europe's notable psychiatrists,

---

[7] Dr. Karl A. Menninger, *Man against Himself* (New York: Harcourt, Brace & Co., 1938), p. 362.

writes: "On the basis of my experience as a psychotherapist, I can state that a large percentage of nervous diseases are illnesses of the conscience."

Few novelists or dramatists have illustrated the devastating effects of guilty feelings so unerringly as Shakespeare in his tragedies. One instance will suffice. The scene is laid on the eve of the Battle of Bosworth Field. King Richard III, laden with guilt because of his enormous crimes, is soliloquizing:

> My conscience hath a thousand several tongues,
> And every tongue brings in a several tale,
> And every tale condemns me for a villain.
> Perjury, perjury, in the high'st degree;
> Murder, stern murder, in the dir'st degree;
> All several sins, all used in each degree;
> Throng to the bar, crying all, "Guilty! guilty!"—
> I shall despair.[8]

An awakened conscience when disregarded will take revenge on body and mind. "When I declared not my sin," says the Psalmist, "my body wasted away" (32:3, freely translated).

While our Lord was ministering to the multitude in Capernaum (Luke 5:18-26), a group of four men brought a sick friend on a stretcher and lowered him down at the feet of Jesus. He lay there a physical wreck, filled with guilty feelings and fears. An insidious disease had been working on his nervous system. Our Lord looked down at that palsied body lying before Him and saw beyond the withered limbs "a servitude of soul." Nineteen centuries before the word "psychosomatic" had been coined by medical science, Jesus was aware that behind this physical sickness lay a moral malady.

Let us be clear on one point: there is plenty of palsy existing today which has no relationship to moral wrongdoing. But in this instance our Lord's diagnosis was correct—these two, a moral malady and a physical malady, were definitely linked in the relationship of cause and effect. It has often been suggested that only the

---

[8] *Richard III*, Act V, Scene 3.

faith of the four friends called forth the sympathy of the Master:
"And seeing *their* faith." But by what right are we to suppose that
the invalid was an indifferent or a reluctant participant in this moving scene? The "their" doubtless included the man on the stretcher.
We can picture him looking up with pitiful and beseeching eyes—
eyes that mirrored a true repentance—into the face of Jesus.

The Great Physician addressed himself to the deepest need in the
life of the helpless invalid—deliverance from his guilty fears. "Son,"
he said, "be of good courage, your sins are forgiven." It was a
physical healing that they desired for the palsied man. But our Lord
directed His healing powers to the primary and basic need in the
man's life. It was only after his life had been flooded with the peace
and joy of the divine forgiveness that our Lord said, "Arise, take up
thy bed and walk."

Sir William Osler, who never failed to note spiritual analogies to
medical science, wrote: "Confession becomes a vaccine against all
morbid poisons left in the system by the infections of yesterday."

The man who in sincere repentance confesses his wrongdoing and
manifests a willingness to make whatever restitution lies in his power
is entitled to a second chance.

As one looks over this vast American civilization so strenuous
and competitive with its teeming millions of people crowded together
in great cities, one need stands out beyond all others—the need of
inner harmony of mind and spirit.

The English poet W. H. Auden tells us that this period of human
history should be called "the Age of Anxiety." Before challenging
this statement, so far as this nation is concerned, it would be well for
us to study the faces of people in any great population center like
New York. Sit in an automobile beside the curb of a busy street, or
in a bus, a subway, a train, or a plane, and watch the faces of
people. You will see there the unmistakable evidence of anxiety and
inner strain and, not seldom, fear.

A little time ago a popular American picture magazine published
a large close-up photograph of a New York crowd hurrying across
the street at 42nd Street and Fifth Avenue. Many people who looked

at this picture were shocked to find in so many faces the expression of crass fear. Modern faces portray many diverse emotions but seldom do they manifest inner harmony of mind and spirit. One reason why multitudes of people are burdened to a greater or less degree by feelings of guilt and fear is because of the difficulty they experience in getting along with other people. There are too many interpersonal conflicts. Again, they are wearied with the pressures and competition of life. It takes a toll of their strength of mind and heart.

The deepest need of people today is to know that they have restored or found fellowship with God. Then they no longer feel alienated from their fellow men. The chief mission of the Church of Jesus Christ is to bring to men and women the healing and the peace of God. John Henry Jowett[9] put it this way: "Out of the church must go forth vigorous healthy men and women who went in maimed and paralyzed. Broken things that no one could mend have been made whole again." Even though a physical malady should remain, strength and grace are given to us by which we can triumph over it, as Paul gloried in his victory over his "thorn in the flesh."

Here then is the mystery of forgiveness—an undeserved mercy on which we cast ourselves, an unmerited grace in which we can put our trust. We don't have to win the favor of God, to plead with Him, to cajole Him, to purchase His forgiveness. The door of His divine mercy is wide open. It was the pierced hand of Christ that opened it. There is a love that does not have to wait for our reformation but stands ready to accept us just as we are—to forgive and to redeem us.

> Nothing in my hand I bring,
> Simply to Thy cross I cling.

In the words of John Bunyan: "So I saw in my dream that just as Christian came up with the cross, his burden loosed from off his shoulder, and fell from off his back and began to tumble and so

[9] Pastor of the Fifth Avenue Presbyterian Church (1911-18), New York.

continued to do, till it came to the mouth of the sepulchre where it fell in, and I saw it no more. Then was Christian glad . . . and said, . . . 'He has given me . . . life by His death.' "

On one occasion at the close of a morning service a member of the congregation who was a stranger to me asked for an interview. She said, "It's rather urgent. If possible at all I should like very much to see you tomorrow." At the appointed time she arrived in the counseling room of our church and her first words to me were: "I came to your church on Sunday not entirely on my own volition. I have been for about a year now a patient in a well-known psychiatric clinic in Hartford, Connecticut, because of a deep depression that has robbed my life of every vestige of joy. I overheard one physician say that I am suffering from a mild case of melancholia. At a later date another mentioned 'manic-depressive psychosis.' I do not know whether or not he was talking about me but these technical terms frightened me badly. The superintendent told me that I can go home for several months and be under the care of our local doctor and then report to him again. 'On your way,' he added, 'I want you to attend a church in New York.' Then he named this church. When I inquired why he wished me to do this, he replied, 'I ask you to do this because one often hears about the forgiveness of sins in that church. This I believe is your greatest need right now. Perhaps the minister there can help you at the point where we failed.' "

The sequel is that several interviews followed, in one of which after a severe mental struggle this woman poured forth a confession of failure as a wife and mother. She had flagrantly betrayed the trust her loved ones had placed in her and could not bring herself to tell the sordid story to anyone other than a pastor who could bring to her an assurance of the divine forgiveness. The effect of her confession and her unreserved acceptance of God's forgiveness was nothing less than extraordinary. Within twenty-four hours the cloud of depression which had enveloped her life for over two years was lifted and she rejoiced in her new-found peace of mind and heart. There has been no recurrence over the last six years. A month after these interviews in New York, on my advice, she returned to the Connecticut clinic for a check-up. After forty-eight hours she was given a discharge with the assurance that she had completely recovered her mental health.

What does God's forgiveness do for the penitent? When an honest confession has been made, whether in the privacy of one's own soul or in the presence of an understanding Christian witness such as a pastor and we have told all of our sins to God, the miracle happens. God forgives our sins and blots them out as though they never had been committed. The Scripture says that He destroys our sins. He wipes them out. He obliterates them. He puts an ocean over them. He separates them from us as far as the east is from the west. In that moment, the debt is canceled. The shackles that bound us are broken. The prisoner is released and goes forth a free man.

One of the greatest contributions that can be made to this modern age for the physical and mental well-being of multitudes is to lead people into an experience of deliverance from guilt. The word "holy" is out of fashion today and yet it is from the Anglo-Saxon "halig": to be whole, to be wholesome, to be healthy.

Every service of worship should afford to the worshiper the unfailing benefit of an experience of group therapy. We should emerge from such a service, if we have engaged in it truly, inwardly renewed, forgiven, cleansed, restored, empowered, with transparent souls, like a clear window through which the light of God may shine.

William James oftentimes said to his students: There is no impression without expression. Certainly Jesus challenged the impotent man by the Pool of Bethesda to express his new-found life. "Rise," he said. "Rise to your feet and manifest your self-respect. Take up your bed. Carry the thing that carried you. Remove this symbol of your weakness, passivity, and inaction." As Marcus Dods put it: "Make no provision for a relapse."

A distinguished professor of medicine from one of the best-known medical clinics in the world came to my counseling room one day following a long-distance call for an appointment. He was a remarkable looking person, immaculately dressed, with an air of distinction about him which attracted the notice even of passersby. Nevertheless when he entered the room his face bore signs of deep trouble and anguish of spirit.

"I have come quite a distance to ask your help. May I now propose one or two questions? Is it possible for a sense of guilt produced by actual wrongdoing to have an adverse effect on one physically and mentally so that one may become unable effectively to do his work?"

I assured him that in my pastoral counseling I had repeatedly met instances of this.

"And now for my second question," he said. "Is it possible to gain an assurance of God's forgiveness so that the burden of guilt will be lifted from one's conscience with a resultant healing of body, mind, and spirit?" I replied that I had known this to happen on many occasions. "Then let us kneel in prayer together," said the medical scientist. He proceeded to offer one of the humblest and most moving prayers I have ever heard as he pleaded for God's forgiveness and pledged his life in new devotion and obedience to Him.

I brought to him the assurance of the Scriptures that God blots out all our transgressions and will remember them no more against us forever; that His divine power will bring to every truly penitent soul new life and healing.

When we rose from our knees the doctor's radiant face was eloquent testimony that the work of healing and restoration had already begun.

The sequel to the interview is worth reporting. On each anniversary of this date, for seven successive years, the medical scientist returned hundreds of miles to New York for the sole purpose of thanking God for the healing which had been wrought in his life. At no time did he make an audible confession of wrongdoing though the mood of contrition was plainly implied by his attitude and questions. Apparently he possessed a faith sufficiently strong so that after silent confession directly to God he could accept without reservation the divine promise of forgiveness and healing.

In many instances men and women of weaker faith find is necessary to confess their sins audibly to a pastor or a Christian friend in order, through personal humiliation, to obtain a complete catharsis and the assurance of divine forgiveness. I used the words "Christian" friend intentionally. At the commencement of my ministry I heard a noted Scottish theologian speaking on this theme. He said, "Never show your wounds to any but a healer." I have never forgotten his counsel.

The physician of the body can improve our physical health. The physician of the mind can minister to our mental well-being. But only the Great Physician himself can unify and harmonize body, mind, and spirit into one integrated whole.

5

Healing and Mental Illness

ONLY IN THE last half-century has the general public begun to adopt a civilized and intelligent attitude toward mental illness. Even today there persists a feeling among a considerable segment of the population in every land that mental sickness is a thing apart from all other illnesses. They believe that it is different in kind from pneumonia or tuberculosis or diabetes; that there is something inherently shameful about it as, for instance, with venereal disease. Prejudice, misunderstanding, and ignorance are not quickly dissipated.

If the truth be known, even among educated people there still lingers a notion that mental illness is a mysterious and much-to-be-dreaded malady that carries a stigma. Members of the clergy are frequently unprepared to deal with the situation when a parishioner falls victim to it. They have the feeling that this is a realm where they have no competence and that their intrusion into it will be resented by physicians and psychiatrists. Clergy and laymen alike are inclined to think that patients in a mental hospital are so withdrawn from reality that they are incapable of grasping religious ideas. On one occasion a college graduate asked me naïvely, "Why do they hold religious services in mental hospitals? They surely don't expect the patients to be interested."

Actually a mental patient is urgently in need of the same attention that is lavished on other sick persons. He is entitled to understanding and tender loving care. He should not be abandoned by his friends, his family, and especially his pastor even though, because of his illness, his behavior and speech may be erratic. Yet this is the undeserved fate that befalls thousands of mentally ill persons all across America. As a consequence they spend many lonely days and nights brooding over the fact that all connections with their former day-by-day life and friendships have been severed, perhaps forever. An additional consideration, very frequently overlooked, is that when these patients recover and are discharged from the hospital their adjustment to life outside the institution and with former friends and acquaintances is made much more difficult because of the rupture in these relationships during their illness.

A present-day pastor is quite correct in asserting that it takes specialized training to deal adequately with mental patients and that as much harm as good may be done through injudicious meddling in their affairs. We are not, however, suggesting the pastor should attempt to assume the role of the physician or psychiatrist but, rather, that he should continue to be a pastor to all members of his flock even though they may be so unfortunate as to become mentally ill.

The ideal situation would be that which infrequently occurs when a psychiatrist has also had some training in theology. A divinity student talked with me at the close of one of my lectures on counseling at Princeton Theological Seminary. He asked, "What would you think of my going into medicine at the end of my second year in theology, and then training as a psychiatrist?" Knowing something of the fine abilities of this student I replied that I thought it was an excellent idea. That was some years ago. He has been practicing psychiatry for a decade and is doing so with greater success because of the spiritual insights he had gained. A more modest role would have to be carried by the pastor who lacked this psychiatric training. Nevertheless it is a most important role and might well have a conclusive effect on the patient's recovery.

In a ministry to mental patients the pastor should have proper preparation and briefing. No pastor should visit a mental patient before he has discussed his intentions with the psychiatrist or psychiatric nurse who has some personal knowledge of the patient. By such a precaution he would avoid mistakes and be better able to minister to his parishioner at the place of his deepest need. The importance of these considerations has been impressed on me ever more deeply by frequent contacts with mental patients throughout a lifetime.

My father was for forty-six years supervisor of a mental hospital in Canada and gave practically his whole working life to the care of the mentally ill. He began his training as a psychiatric nurse immediately after he had taken on the job of attendant, and interestingly enough to this day he is the only male nurse who has received a diploma from this Canadian institution.[1] From the time I was about twelve years of age the high point of my early life was an occasional weekend spent with my father at this hospital. He would sometimes take me with him on his morning round of the wards when he would dress patients' wounds and talk over with them their complaints and their problems. Occasionally he left me for half an hour on a ward in the care of the attendant while he was engaged elsewhere. I found plenty of entertainment talking with the patients and had a few special friends who always called me by my first name. In these early years I learned to feel completely at ease with the mentally ill.

Later, at the age of seventeen, when I had dropped out of school I persuaded my father to give me a job as an attendant in the hospital. Since I was already more than six feet tall and looked older than my seventeen years, my youthfulness created no special problem. I worked alternately on the twelve- and fifteen-hour day with one day off in thirteen. The salary, incidentally, was $17 per month. My chief employment was the oversight of a patient who was a lawyer and under conviction for embezzlement. He had been pronounced insane by a jury that had listened to psychiatric testimony. His restless, brilliant mind made him a considerable problem to the attendants. He became impatient with them because of their lack of con-

[1] Falconwood Hospital, presently known as Riverside Hospital, Charlottetown, Prince Edward Island, Canada.

versational ability. Several of them also had been in the habit of
asking him to read aloud to them from worthless books. My success
in dealing with this man was due chiefly to the fact that I had sought
his help in tutoring me for college entrance. He welcomed the opportunity for mental exercise. His illness, which had been diagnosed as
paranoia,[2] interfered in no way whatsoever with his memory, his
intelligence, or his tutoring ability. He was one of the most brilliant
men I have ever known.

At the same time for a period of two and a half years I took the
lectures on psychiatric nursing given by the medical superintendent
and gained insights and understanding that could scarcely have been
acquired in any other way. While considerable progress has been
made psychiatrically since that time, I gained practical experience
and an understanding of human personality that ever since has been
a priceless asset to me. Many years later, while I was senior pastor
of the Fifth Avenue Presbyterian Church, I was invited to address a
meeting of a psychiatric society in New York. The members informed me that in twenty-five years I was the only clergyman who
had ever addressed them. Needless to say this fact did not put me
more at ease. I chose the topic "Spiritual Therapy." About a score
of psychiatrists commented on my paper and their remarks were
generally in a friendly vein. The chief psychiatrist of a large and well-
known New York mental hospital in the course of his remarks said
something that I have never forgotten. "We psychiatrists," he said,
"must admit that we know all too little about mental illness in its
acute forms. The only people who really have a knowledge of mental
illness at its deepest level are those who have had an opportunity to
observe closely the patients. Like our reader [i.e., lecturer], they
have lived and eaten and slept on the wards with their patients. I
refer to the attendants. These people could teach us much if they had
the education and the intellectual capacity to note what was happening around them and then to report it accurately. This is the service
that our reader for tonight has rendered to us." During two and a

_____

[2] Systematized delusions of persecution.

half years in the Canadian mental hospital I was able to acquire knowledge and insights into life and the behavior of people that I could never have gleaned in a comparable period in any university.

I frankly confess that during those years of training I did not have in mind the noble purpose of gaining psychiatric knowledge in order to serve my fellow men. At the beginning I wanted only a job and thought little of the benefits that might accrue to me or to others. It was the patient under my care, this very able Canadian lawyer, who opened my eyes to the implications of what was going on around me and brought clearly to my attention the insights and understanding that could be gained from my work. On one occasion he said to me, "If you should decide to go into the ministry I trust that you will not forget what you have seen in this institution and that you will further develop the understanding you have gained in dealing with those who are mentally ill. If you can learn to combine the knowledge you are gaining here with the power of religion to stabilize human minds, you will blaze trails."

Hospital chaplains and pastors who seek to improve their abilities as spiritual counselors should not conclude too readily that mental patients are unreachable by religious therapy. They may be helped even though they have given no slightest evidence that contact has been established with them. My father out of his wealth of experience often reminded me that though a man may be mentally ill he is not necessarily immune to help. More than a half-century ago he was constantly urging the authorities to appoint carefully selected and well-trained chaplains in all mental hospitals. "Faith exerts a power," he said to me, "that reaches past all the barriers erected by mental diseases, and ministers to the mind and soul of man in his extremity."

In my own ministry I have met notable illustrations of the validity of my father's teaching. Shortly after coming to New York I formed a deep and lasting friendship with a well-known physician. Once every week for a period of several years we met for a two-hour luncheon to talk over subjects of mutual interest. At my friend's suggestion we established what was virtually a service of Holy

Communion. In most instances this impressive rite was performed monthly in his private office on Park Avenue. Always he kept a bottle of sacramental wine available and three highly prized glasses that were more than a century old. Each of us poured wine in one glass for ourselves and the third was placed in the center of the table as a reminder of the Unseen Guest. In the service of Holy Communion, after we had partaken of the bread and wine, each in turn drank from the larger glass which represented the presence of the Unseen Guest. We concluded by repeating together the Lord's Prayer. This simple service was always a deeply moving experience.

Out of it came a covenant of friendship. If one of us at any time in the future should be in any kind of difficulty or distress the other would at once come to his assistance. When my medical friend retired to California we saw each other at intervals of approximately two years. On each of these occasions we unfailingly celebrated our rite of friendship and Holy Communion. A year or two after our last meeting I was shocked to learn that he had suffered a cerebral hemorrhage some time earlier and was in a private hospital for mental cases on the Pacific coast. As soon as possible I took a plane to California and went to the hospital where my friend was a patient. Arriving there I asked to see the medical superintendent and inquired about my friend. This was his reply: "About a year ago, following a severe cerebral hemorrhage, your friend began to deteriorate very rapidly. The situation has been complicated by the fact that he is suffering from advanced arteriosclerosis. After the rupture of a blood vessel partial paralysis set in. He could no longer walk without the assistance of two people. He became confused and disorientated. He cannot now recall either recent or remote memories." He added that the latter ability is usually the last to go. The superintendent continued, "When his son and daughter visited him a week apart he did not recognize either of them. He is now totally careless of his appearance. Indeed as a person he is completely beyond our reach." I told the superintendent about our pledge to each other and his reply was that my visit would be fruitless and also that it would be a most distressing experience for me to see my friend's present condition. "It would be best, I think, for you to have the memory of him as you knew him a few years ago." I informed the superintendent that throughout my ministry I have had some unusual experiences of reaching people who appeared to be beyond the help of therapy and in some cases were even in a coma, and assured him that I still wished to visit my friend. He gave me a somewhat reluctant consent.

The head nurse escorted me to a small room in which were two chairs and a table. Shortly, I heard the shuffling of feet and a couple of nurses entered the room, supporting a man who appeared unable even to stand unassisted. For a moment I thought that they had brought in the wrong patient, as I could see no resemblance to my friend in this man. Physically, he seemed to have lost height. His face was shrunken and wrinkled like an ancient parchment and he was bent over as though with a spinal affliction. When the nurses had left I asked my friend if he knew me, and gave the nickname by which he had known me. He peered intently into my face and said, "No, I don't believe I have ever met you before." I repeated my name but it aroused no response from him. I asked about his children. He replied he had not seen them in years. While my friend was watching me I opened a briefcase and produced a linen napkin and spread it on the table. I took out three glasses, some wafers, and a bottle of sacramental wine. As I carefully poured the wine into the three glasses, I saw that for the first time he was becoming interested. I said to him, "Remember, the third glass is for the Unseen Guest. Christ is with us here as he has promised and we are now about to perform our ritual of friendship." As I recited the service of Holy Communion, at the end of each collect he joined me in saying "Amen." We both partook of the broken bread and the wine, and then each of us in turn drank from the third glass. Then, as our custom was, I repeated slowly and clearly the Lord's Prayer, and I was gratified to hear him phrase by phrase repeating the words with me right to the end of the prayer. Again I mentioned the nickname by which he had known me. His eyes lighted up and he responded,

"Are you really Sid? You must be because only you would have known of this ceremony." Then I reminded him of the pledge we had made that either one of us would come to the other in his hour of need. I added, "That is why I am here today." He reached out and took my hand and said with deep feeling, "When you put it like that it brings tears to my eyes."

This spiritual fellowship awakened memories of the past and we shared a number of experiences that we had had together. Knowing that he had but a brief time to live, I promised my friend that I would contact a minister in the nearby city and ask him to make regular pastoral visits to the hospital. After a further conversation and prayer we had an affectionate parting and I went off to catch my plane to New York. This experience, along with other similar ones, though none quite as dramatic as this, further reinforced in my mind my father's words, "Faith exerts a power that reaches past all the barriers erected by mental diseases and ministers to the mind and soul of man in his extremity."

It is important for anyone, minister or layman, who visits a mental hospital to keep in mind that mental illness may be of many different types and degrees of severity. Some patients may be highly dangerous to themselves and to others. Always there are a few suicidal and homicidal patients on the wards. It would be a vast mistake to judge any mental patient merely by a benevolent appearance. On one occasion when I was fourteen years old and spending a weekend with my father, I attended a chapel service. After the service was dismissed by the visiting preacher I was accosted by a white-haired kind-looking old man who apparently was a patient. He said to me, "You are, I believe, the supervisor's son, aren't you? Well I hope that you will grow up to be a fine man like your father. It always pays," he added, "to obey the Lord's commandments."

I noticed that my father was looking intently in our direction while the old man was talking with me. Afterward as we were going down the elevator to my father's office, I said to him, "Why do you keep that nice old man locked up in the hospital? He seems perfectly all right." My father replied, "I saw him talking to you. I don't want you ever to be with that man alone. Six months ago he found a loose floor board under the bathtub in his ward. He pried it out and used it to kill another patient about whom he had a delusion." "Why in the world do you suppose he would do a thing like that?" I asked my father. His reply was, "He told me that God had commanded him to destroy that man. He said that he was only executing God's order." That shocker experienced in my teens taught me an unforgettable lesson: that I should never make too quick an assumption about any mental patient.

Even when I had become an attendant at the hospital and had begun my studies under the medical superintendent, I still found it difficult to accept the fact that certain patients in the institution were mentally ill. My greatest difficulty lay with the lawyer who was my special patient. His mind was so richly stored with knowledge and he expressed it all with such logic and clarity that I found it exceedingly difficult to accept the psychiatric diagnosis that he was insane. Time and again I would argue his case with my father, not having the courage to take the matter up with the medical superintendent. Patiently my father would explain that deep down within the unconscious of this man there were grave disorders. Only at the deepest levels of his mind and in matters that concerned himself intimately could these aberrations in his thinking be perceived. By the time I left the hospital I understood my patient much better and found that I could handle him by writing suggestions to him in a difficult code and then letting him discover them in a supposedly accidental fashion. He would not accept suggestions offered to him directly and simply. Everything had to be deep and mysterious.

Earlier in this chapter I referred to some of the reasons why I succeeded with my special patient but omitted one of the most important reasons of all. Only rarely did this lawyer-patient talk to me about his ideas of God. When he did so usually he related his thoughts to the fact that there was a possibility I might enter the Christian ministry. He very seldom even hinted at the offenses for which he had been convicted. But on one occasion he opened up and expressed his thoughts more freely. He said to me, "You see, I have some debts to pay, an obligation to society and to God. I feel that these debts are going to be very difficult for me to discharge. I have been in this institution now for four years and there is little prospect of my being released any time soon, for the tide of public opinion is running strong against me. You will not be staying here. You are not intended for this kind of job. There is a bigger world waiting for you. If I can be of any help in training you for college so that the way may be opened for you to become a minister, in some measure at least I shall be helping to discharge my debt both to society and to God."[3]

One day my patient turned to me and asked abruptly, "If you should find yourself a patient some day in this hospital and you had to appear before a group of physicians whose task it was to determine whether or not you were a legally sane or insane person, how would you go about defending yourself and proving your sanity?" I asked him why he had brought up this question. He replied that this had happened to one of the patients on his ward. Two doctors had come in to question him at the insistence of his family. This fellow patient told him how he had responded. He had said to the doctors, "I defy any man or woman alive to point to one insane act that I have ever committed or one insane word I have ever used."

"Now," said my patient, "that was not the best way to establish his sanity. It was of course the natural and inevitable way in which most people in his situation would react."

"Well how would you go about defending yourself," I asked him.

"Well my best plan would be not to volunteer any statements or opinions or protestations, but simply to answer as reasonably as I could any questions that the doctors would ask me," he replied. He did not pursue the matter any further but this bit of conversation reveals how carefully he had thought through all aspects of the problems facing a mental patient.

On occasion I used to talk to my father about his experiences

[3] See Bonnell, *Pastoral Psychiatry* (New York: Harper & Row, 1938), p. 25.

when he began his course of training in this hospital. "Even in my lifetime," he would say, "there has been a great change in the attitude toward and the treatment of mental patients." His own experience went back to the last quarter of the nineteenth century. "There was a time," he said, "when people who were mentally sick were treated as wild animals that had forcibly to be restrained. They were ridiculed and teased and made the object of sport by their tormentors. They were also, of course, frequently beaten severely. If they were subject to periods of violence, however, they were greatly feared."

It is not difficult to discover the reasons why feelings of shame in some degree still adhere to various forms of mental illness when we remember that in earlier centuries insanity was thought to be a form of demoniacal possession. It was only when medical science had reached a certain point in its progress that it was able to challenge these superstitious ideas, and mental illness began to be accepted as a natural result of physical and psychological disorders.

Strangely enough, when we look back into history we discover that in the pre-Christian era and for a century or two afterward, among the Greeks and Romans, the insane were treated with far greater understanding and kindliness than they were from the Middle Ages up to the close of the nineteenth century. Hippocrates of Cos (460?-377? B.C.), the father of medicine, had the insight and the good sense to declare that insanity is simply a disease of the brain. By the time of Galen (A.D. c.130-c.200), enlightened physicians generally urged that the insane be regarded as sick people and treated with care and kindness, instead of inflicting imprisonment, beatings, and torture on them.

Unfortunately side by side with these praiseworthy developments there came to the fore in the Christian Church prelates who pushed aside the noble achievements of the Greek and Roman physicians and gave their sanction to superstitious ideas that madness and demonic possession were almost identical terms. That this viewpoint was also general in Jesus' day is made clear by assertions found in many places in the New Testament. One of these occurs in John's

Gospel (10:20) where it was said by the opponents of our Lord, "He hath a devil and is mad; why hear ye him?" These ideas recorded in ancient writings of the fathers of the Christian Church have now come to have a ludicrous aspect for modern people. For instance the learned St. Gregory the Great solemnly relates this story: "A nun having eaten some lettuce without the sign of the cross swallowed a devil and when commanded by a holy man to come forth the devil replied 'How am I to blame? I was sitting on the lettuce and this woman not having made the sign of the cross ate me along with it.' "[4]

The cruelties oftentimes visited upon the insane were due to the theory that a satanic or demonic presence in them should be severely punished in the hope of freeing the victim of these evil spirits. Those who devised this dreadful mode of treatment believed also that all demons were guilty of pride and the only way to expel them from a human being was to humiliate them. Consequently, the *Treasury of Exorcisms*[5] is packed with the vilest epithets that one could possibly conjure up. These were believed to be the proper words with which to address the demons in the insane man. Many of these terms are unprintable. A few that could be mentioned at all are these: "Thou lustful and stupid one, thou wrinkled beast, thou mangy beast, thou beast of all beasts the most beastly, thou filthy sow, thou envious crocodile, swollen toad, entangled spider, etc., etc.," The insane even in the age of Charlemagne were jailed, whipped, forced to drink noxious emetics, to inhale fumes of brimstone, and to suffer other unspeakable indignities in the hope of freeing them from the demons that possessed them.

Even the best of men in those days were caught up in this false interpretation. Sir Thomas More, for instance, ordered that lunatics be publicly whipped.[6] Shakespeare, too, reveals the prevalence of

[4] *Exempla* of Archbishop Jacque deVitry, edited by T. F. Crane, p. 15, as quoted by White, *op. cit.*, Vol. II, p. 101.

[5] *Thesaurus Exorcismorum* (Cologne, 1626), as quoted by White, *op. cit.*, Vol. II, p. 107.

[6] D. H. Tuke, *History of the Insane in the British Isles*, pp. 63-73; as quoted

these ideas, for he makes one of his characters refer to madmen as deserving "a dark house and a whip."[7] Is it any wonder, therefore, that up to the close of the nineteenth century mental patients were often treated as outcasts and their presence in a family was frequently regarded as a judgment of God. In the light of past history it is understandable also that a sense of revulsion, contempt, or fear should still be manifested by a proportion of people in our own day who are not versed in the history of mental illness.

To France must go the major credit for leading the whole world in a new and enlightened treatment of the insane. The man who pioneered in this movement was Dr. Jean Baptiste Pinel. In 1792 he was made superintendent of a huge mental hospital at Bicêtre. There he discarded all cruelties visited upon the insane and claimed that their affliction was simply a bodily disease. The reign of diabolism was coming to an end. "For the brutality and cruelty which had prevailed up to that time, Pinel substituted kindness and gentleness. Patients were taken out of the dungeons and given sunny rooms and allowed the liberty of pleasant grounds for exercise; chains were thrown aside. At the same time the mental power of each patient was developed by its fitting exercise and the disease was met with remedies sanctioned by experiment, observation and reason."[8] The news of this great medical advance swept across Europe and a new era opened for multitudes of unfortunate human beings.

My father commenced to work in the field of mental illness about the time that many of these improvements began to appear on the American continent and a kindly attitude toward the insane was winning general acceptance. Nevertheless, even as late as the '80s and '90s severe restraints were still put on patients. Oftentimes those who were disturbed or "violent" were placed in strongly built boxes

---

in White, A History of the Warfare of Science with Religion in Christendom (New York: D. Appleton Co., 1897), Vol. II, p. 41.

[7] As You Like It, Act III, Scene 2.

[8] Comments by Dr. Andrew D. White, former president and professor of history at Cornell University. From A History of the Warfare of Science with Theology in Christendom, op. cit., Vol. II, p. 131.

that resembled coffins. The cover was hinged and padlocked and there were slats to let in the air so that the patient would not suffocate. Many times in his earlier experiences my father said that he would be awakened at night by the rattling of the lids on these boxes. Gradually he saw disappearing the padded cell, the strait-jacket, and the harsh treatment. Next came hydrotherapy, oftentimes in the form of prolonged hot baths that soothed disturbed patients. Finally, we have today various tranquilizers that quiet the most violent and that enable the psychiatrist to begin therapeutic interviews with these sick persons. I was unfailingly impressed by the respect which my father had for the mentally ill. He would talk with them as with a normal individual, and listen patiently to them when they told him of their delusions and hallucinations. He had a quiet habit of asking patients on the wards why they expressed certain ideas and telling them to explain to him how they reached these conclusions. I noticed that little by little as they attempted this explanation some of them would get insight into their fallacious modes of reasoning.

Many persons who deal with the mentally ill are quite unaware of how sensitive they are to the reactions of other people. They are grievously hurt if people are amused at what they say or laugh at some of their incongruous ideas, or try too insistently to point out the falsity of their reasoning. This simply means that the patient is repelled by these persons and they lose the opportunity they might have had for helping him. When a pastor goes to a mental hospital to visit a parishioner he should talk naturally to him. Of course when he is asked questions he should answer them just as he would in the case of a person who is sane. He will not, however, supply any family information that might gravely disturb the patient. He should listen much and speak little. The capacity to listen attentively, sympathetically, is one of the most important qualities in a counselor or pastor. When a pastor converses with the mentally ill he should not be offended by any remarks the patient makes concerning the pastor, his family or the members of his church. He should listen patiently to the criticisms, the complaints, the hopes and fears of the sick man.

It is important also that the pastor not deepen the patient's sense of guilt. If he wishes to confess certain acts of wrongdoing the pastor will of course lead him into an experience of God's forgiveness. In conversation with the mentally ill he should be hopeful, optimistic within reason, and reassuring. Even if no confession of guilt is made the pastor should from time to time speak of the reality of God's forgiveness. Comments such as these may oftentimes draw forth a confession from the patient. He should never make light of any anxieties and fears or any statement made by the patient about his inner suffering as though these were unimportant. He will endeavor to establish an empathic relationship with the patient as he talks of the ordeal through which he is passing. Compassion should be the pastor's chief characteristic.

One reason some people have felt it inadvisable that religious services be held for mental patients is their fear that it might leave them worse off than before. However, experiences both within mental hospitals and outside them indicate quite the reverse.

The value of religious ministries to a mental patient is seen in an episode related by the Rev. Dr. Anton T. Boisen.[9] It is a case history of a man to whom he gives the name of Rudolph. This patient, Dr. Boisen tells us, was under a severe strain of anxiety with respect to his past life and his sins. The patient had been spending many nights in prayer and tears. Then came the unforgettable occasion when he went to hear Dwight L. Moody preach. Moody talked about God as the Heavenly Father who is ready to blot out all our transgressions and give us a new life. Said Rudolph, "It was a natural phenomenon that came over me. I had gone there a downcast individual, not a young man but an old man. When I came out I felt as though the very sparrows in the trees were singing songs. Every-

[9] See *Religion in Crisis and Custom* (New York: Harper & Row, 1945), pp. 48-52.

thing was changed. It seemed such a real experience. . . . I was happy for many years after that and I was more successful in my work."

Dr. Boisen stresses the fact that this man was really in grave peril. At that very moment he was a candidate for a mental hospital and in a state of anxiety which might easily have passed into acute panic. In Rudolph's own words he suffered "unspeakable worry." Dr. Boisen points out that the immediate effect of this experience of forgiveness was a release of tension. The man felt himself absolved directly by God. He had now a new role in life. He had something to live and work for.

This type of experience is not unknown to counselors, especially those who are religiously motivated. Of course when one is dealing with an acute crisis of anxiety he must be aware of the factors involved in the situation. When an actual psychotic condition may be in the offing it would be wise to leave such cases in the hands of psychiatrists or experienced and well-trained pastors. However, every pastor would do well in the visitation of mental patients either in his conversation or prayers to make mention of the Great Physician who lifts from our hearts the burden of anxieties and sins.

One of the most dramatic and unforgettable experiences of my entire ministry was in this area so fraught with possibilities for good or ill.[10] On three successive Sundays a well-dressed man came up at the end of the line of people with whom I was talking and asked for a private interview. It was not until after his third visit that I was able to see him. It was indicative of his need for help that he had taken a two-hour journey by train to reach our church. Evidently he was in serious trouble. It was only a matter of weeks since he had been discharged from a mental hospital in the hope that he would be able to work at his profession at least two hours a day. He found himself unable to resume his work at all. His stay in the mental

[10] This incident is mentioned in my book *Psychology for Pastor and People* (New York: Harper & Row, 1960), pp. 110-111.

hospital continued for almost twelve months. He had received more than twenty electroshock treatments. He told me that he'd rather die than submit again to this form of therapy. The one glimmer of hope that kept him from complete despair was his hearing a radio address I had given on the subject of God's forgiveness. I soon discovered that he had not played fair with the psychiatrist in the hospital, for he had withheld a story of moral wrongdoing. It became evident after one or two interviews that all the threads in the black web of mental depression were tied up in this moral defeat of earlier years. Even the mental illness was self-punishment for wrongdoing that had remained unconfessed and unforgiven. The conflict between his high moral standards and the knowledge of his own inner failure and defeat had become too much for him so he had retreated into the wilderness of a psychosis.

This married man with a family poured out the humiliating confession that he had kept lodged in his breast for a decade. He had been guilty of repeated infidelities. The crisis was reached when it became apparent that all his misdeeds might soon be published in the press because of threatened legal action. This dire happening did not come to pass, but he was emotionally shattered by the fear of it. During all these ten years none of his friends suspected that concealed under a placid exterior were inner conflicts and deep anxieties that tortured him. On his journeys to New York to see me, after he left the mental hospital, he was always accompanied by his wife. She, too, knew nothing of the secret roots of his trouble. He was afraid to travel alone either by train or by taxi and could not walk in the street without resting at the end of each block because of the violent palpitation of his heart. Sometimes at night he would wake up with the feeling that he was at the point of death. He suffered from a sense of suffocation and at moments felt that his heart was about to stop beating.

On an eventful visit, after a full and complete confession accompanied by an emotional upheaval, he gratefully accepted the scriptural assurance of divine forgiveness: "I, even I, am He that blotteth out all thy transgressions and I will not remember thy sins" (Isa. 43:25). His whole appearance underwent a change. He became in a very real sense a new man. On this occasion, as usual, his wife was waiting for him on the ground floor. I went down with him on the elevator that took us from the counseling room to the street level and suggested that he should say nothing at all, at first, to his wife about the inner change that had just occurred. She was seated in the waiting room, quietly reading. I walked over and said to her, "Your husband is ready to see you." She got up quickly and walked to the door of the elevator where he was standing. For a brief moment she stood with an amazed expression on her face, looking at him. Then sensing the profound change that had occurred, she ran forward and flinging herself into his arms said, "Darling, you are better now. You will be well, I know it." There were additional interviews after this, to which he now came alone. On the day when the transformation was wrought, which I have just described, he walked twenty-three blocks without resting and was completely free of distressing heart symptoms. Within two months he was working at his profession up to a six-hour day without unusual evidence of fatigue.

Certainly it is true that had this patient made a clean breast to his psychiatrist or to the doctors in the mental hospital they could have done more for him. However, I question seriously whether in this particular situation, given this man's moral outlook, he could have found complete deliverance from the hands of anyone other than a trained pastor-counselor. He needed someone who could say with conviction: "Your sins are forgiven you. I tell you this on the authority of the Word of God." In such happenings it is advisable to give to the patient a verse of Scripture that he can repeat and which will express his gratitude for the inner transformation that has been wrought. For such a person the Psalms are most helpful. The man whom we have been discussing took the following words as his expression of gratitude and repeated them many times a day:

Bless the Lord, O my soul: and all that is within me, bless his holy name.
Bless the Lord, O my soul, and forget not all his benefits:
Who forgiveth all thine iniquities; who healeth all thy diseases;

Who redeemeth thy life from destruction; who crowneth thee with loving
kindness and tender mercies.

Psalm 103:1-4

There are many types of mental illness where the pastor can be
helpful. One of these is "depression." The technical name of this
when it reaches a psychotic stage is "melancholia." Nowadays this
type of illness is chiefly called "manic-depressive psychosis."

While I was serving as a psychiatric nurse in the Canadian hospital to which I have referred, occasionally I had to assume duties on
the grounds. Among the patients allotted to me for trimming the
roads and lawns was a young man about twenty-four years of age. I
had known him slightly in earlier years and was fairly well acquainted with his family. I had him work with me on several occasions but found it very difficult to lead him into a conversation. He
would answer in monosyllables and would not glance in my direction
as he responded to questions. He appeared to have lost interest in
what was happening in the world outside himself. His self-regarding
moods had almost disappeared and I often heard him audibly re-
proaching himself. He seemed to suffer from the delusion that severe
punishment was awaiting him. Although this young man had a good
physique he would complain shortly of being fatigued and express
the wish to be returned to the ward. Always a cloud of sadness
seemed to hang over him. This is true generally of most of these
melancholia patients. I had known that this young man at one time
was quite active in a Protestant church and sometimes served as an
usher. When I asked him to take on an extra duty he invariably
pleaded weariness. He was dominated by a feeling of loneliness and
suffering from the idea that he had been forsaken by his family. I
began to pay particular attention to him in an effort to offset his
feeling of abandonment. After a little time he began to appreciate
these attempts at friendship and made a slow and somewhat inade-
quate response. One day when he became a little more communica-
tive, he said "Nobody, nobody at all has any interest in me." I said,
"You're wrong there. God has never ceased to be interested in you.
Right now his love surrounds you. I'm your friend. I'm interested in

you, and I want to see you get well." For the first time I saw that he was listening. My words apparently had made an impression. A change was in the making. The next time I had him in a work party he was much more responsive. Within two weeks he was conversing with me. One day as we talked together while working, he said to me, "Really I feel that I am brokenhearted with all the calamities that have befallen me, and most of all with my coming into this place. Yes, I'm brokenhearted." Happily there came to my mind a Bible verse (Ps. 147:2-3) which was frequently quoted in our family and I mentioned it to him, though I could not tell him, then, where it was to be found: "The Lord healeth the broken in heart and bindeth up their wounds." He repeated these words several times that day to himself just loud enough for me to overhear. After that we frequently discussed God's care of the individual. He walked erectly now and there was a clear light in his eyes. Within six weeks he was discharged from the hospital. I am convinced that spiritual therapy did as much or even more for this man than medication or work therapy.

Spiritual therapy, as I have already noted, appears to reach down into the inner life of the individual. This is especially true of one who has had a previous experience of genuine religion. The solid fact of an experiential knowledge of God in the past undergirds a human life with a sense of reality despite erratic thoughts and fantasies. He has something to come back to that is sane, enduring, satisfying, real.

It will not be given to every pastor who visits parishioners in mental hospitals to have experiences like some of those I have mentioned. It must be remembered that I had worked with some of these patients for weeks or months. I have recorded several successes but I had failures too, largely due to my inability to reach the inner and well-defended citadel of the patient's life. Nevertheless I am persuaded that the act of friendship in visiting these mental patients cannot be without constructive effects. The pastor's visit can be made a warmly personal experience that will assure his parishioner of his minister's continued interest in him and of the thoughts and prayers of the members of the congregation to which he still belongs. If a patient is seriously ill it would be best for the average pastor to attempt nothing other than to manifest the utmost friendliness toward the parishioner and perhaps offer a brief—very brief—prayer. One of the most enduring results of such a visit is the fact that it is a tentative preparation for the patient's return to his home.

An article appeared in May, 1968, in the *New York Times* with Dr. Howard A. Rusk's by-line, entitled "A New Mental Center." This is how it begins:

If you were a patient in a mental hospital for months or years or decades, your great dream would be to go home. However, you would be frightened, very frightened. You would question yourself with deep anxiety and have inward thoughts of stark fear.

Can I make it? I need more time, more help, more counseling, more understanding if I am going back and make good in this fast-moving, complicated, mixed-up world.

Dr. Rusk then goes on to tell of rehabilitation centers that are now being established—one at Long Island's Central Islip State Hospital, costing $5 million. This new facility will be completed by 1970. It has a swimming pool, bowling alley, auditorium, gymnasium, library, cafeteria, craftshops, etc. There will be group psychotherapy and counseling. It will be built on the hospital grounds near the living quarters of the patients. This is part of New York State's five-year program for improving state mental hospital services. Six other similar rehabilitation centers are being provided.

Dr. Rusk adds: "It is not enough that the patients improve and leave our mental hospitals to return to their homes. We must also take steps prior to their release to prepare them for their return to society." It is most gratifying to know of this very important program now under way, and it will mean much that patients who are nearing the time for discharge can experiment to reacquire their social skills and confidence before they face life in society outside the hospital walls. These halfway houses are very important. Dr. Rusk concludes that "as the patient recovering from physical illness needs physical conditioning, so also the mental patient will need psychological strengthening." The success of the efforts that we make for the patients being discharged from mental hospitals will be determined to a large degree by how we have dealt with them when they were in the hospital.

A little time ago a Royal Commission set up by the Canadian government dealt with the feeling of the general public toward mental illness. It called for "an immediate end to the distinction that some still make in attitudes toward those who are mentally ill and those who are physically ill. Already," the report said, "there is an encouraging trend in this direction, and if this is followed by positive action the outlook for treatment is much more hopeful and may actually be optimistic."

The recommendation made by the Royal Commission is that instead of building separate institutions for the mentally sick in which they will feel dreadfully isolated, those suffering from mental illness should go to a special wing in the general hospital. It is recommended that there be no more than three hundred beds in the psychiatric department. It will make a great difference, the Commission suggested, if this is done rather than isolating the patients in large, segregated "asylums."

One does not have to look back very far to remember a time when a person suffering from mental illness that required hospitalization would find himself cut off from his friends, his relatives, his employers and fellow workers, and all social and church groups. The feeling existed that most of these patients were doomed as incurables. Today, instead of looking upon them as hopeless, we think of them as eminently recoverable and entitled to continuous contact with most of those with whom they were associated before the illness. Oftentimes attempts to keep these mental patients in touch with the society of their fellow citizens have been spearheaded by church groups. It is important that the people to whom they will be returned and with whom they must function in normal life should not be out of touch with them in the hour of their adversity. Not a few ministers are taking special training now so that they can work more effectively with the mentally ill. They are acquiring useful medical information regarding mental illness and developing the qualities of sensitivity and understanding that will make them a prime aid to such helping professionals as the psychiatrists and the psychiatric nurses.

One private psychiatric clinic located a short distance from New York City in a special report states that there has been a very large increase in young patients coming to the clinic. Their ages range from seventeen to twenty-five years. They comprise about one third of the resident patients in the clinic. If it is important that adults be kept in contact with so-called normal friends and people outside the clinic or hospital, this is even more true of young people. It is highly advisable that they do not lose contact with their own age group. Only those who have actually undergone the experience or have seen it close at hand can know how formidable is the task of a mental patient to make a happy readjustment to his family and friends and business associates.

The undertaking has some resemblance to the difficulties encountered by one who has been in military service for five or more years and is suddenly projected into .civilian life. For the mental patient the ordeal is five times greater. Nevertheless, there are similarities between the two. In the mental hospital and in the army somebody else assumes responsibility for the patient's or the soldier's food, lodging, and clothing. He is told when he should arise in the morning and go to bed at night, when he should wash and bathe himself, and many added details of daily life. The decisions in all these matters are in the hands of others.

When a discharged mental patient is faced with the inevitable trials and testings of a competitive society he sometimes longs for the ease and comfort of noncompetitive institutional life. A physician who had spent more than twelve months as a patient in a mental hospital told a colleague that he had to fight with all the willpower he possessed and all the resources of his rationality to keep from returning to the world of unreality where all his battles had been won and the "victories" were cheaply bought. Obstacles that at one time in civilian life he had faced without quailing now towered in his pathway like veritable mountains.

A year or two ago when I was in Australia on a two months' visit a member of a group called Recovery brought certain facts to my attention. The group had its beginning when several of its present members who had been discharged from mental hospitals happened to meet at a group assembly of Alcoholics Anonymous. These few persons were there not because they were alcoholics but because they needed the kind of benefit that A.A. groups could bring to them in the matter of rehabilitation. They discussed when they got together the possibility of starting a group similar to Alcoholics Anonymous but devoted directly to the rehabilitation of persons who had suffered from mental illness. It would be open also to others who were in danger of mental illness. They heard of an organization in the United States called Recovery, Inc., and so they took the name slightly abbreviated and called their group Recovery. Their first meeting was held in 1957. Now there are more than a score of such groups in New South Wales alone. In the matter of membership no one will be barred from the group because of political affiliation, race, religion, social standing, etc. All that is asked is a frank admission of mental illness and a willingness to be helped by fellow sufferers. They learn to treat their illnesses with matter-of-fact openness. It hardly need be said that all confidences revealed at any of the meetings must be kept inviolate by the membership. The members, after the fashion of A.A., are called only by their first names. They seek the removal of the social stigma attached to mental sickness, the unrealism that surrounds it, and the dispelling of an atmosphere of mystery and foreboding. Members are free to discuss their own illness and the ideas that they held then or still hold. Then when they hear others talking about the same problem and how they overcame false notions, they are very greatly helped. It assists them to overcome the idea that they are suffering from some strange and unique malady. They learn, too, to speak with complete frankness of their sickness and to discuss it with others who have also gone through deep waters. As they hear other group members speak of the progress that they have made and the disciplining of their thinking processes they are heartened and inspired. The meetings last for one hour and a half. The procedure for each meeting is for the chairman to ask for a brief silence while all present collect their thoughts and place themselves in the presence of the Supreme Healer. Then after the silence, generally, the chairman recites the following words:

While we place ourselves in the presence of the Supreme Healer for the work of this meeting let us not think only of our own individual needs but let us also invoke His guidance and help
—for ALL Recovery members here present
—for absent members from the Group who may need our prayers at this moment
—and for all our fellow mental suffers in hospitals or wherever else they may be.

It has been found that when some members of the group bring to a meeting somebody who is in a serious nervous condition and threatened with mental illness he is often helped and greatly relieved to hear his own problem talked out by other persons. The definition given by Recovery to mental health is: "The vigor and peace of mind of one wholly attuned to reality." It should not need to be said, of course, that this group works as a supplement to the efforts of medical men. Sometimes doctors conversant with mental illness are called in to speak briefly. Most patients emerge from treatment in mental hospitals as one of their number has put it "stunned and shaken." They are troubled by what some of them describe as "an emotional hangover." They have a sense of shock, of personal injury, and generally a feeling of rebellion against society. If they have been under a considerable amount of drug therapy this too militates against recovery because they now have to fight the battle for mastery of the desire for drugs, with its resultant neurotic dependence.

In mental illness, too, the will to recover is most important. The members of these Recovery groups say that in order to get well every mentally ill person must have the will to get well. The truth is, they tell us, that many sick persons would like to get well but are unwilling to do what is necessary for recovery. They dislike changing, going against their feelings, and they shrink back from the effort of facing responsibilities that must be assumed when they recover.

They must also be ready to give up the special attention and kindly interest that has been shown them because of their mental illness. They will need the strengthening and stabilizing power of prayer. At this point we do well to recall the familiar words of Dr. Alexis Carrel, Nobel prize winner and author of the book, *Man the Unknown:* "When we pray we link ourselves with the inexhaustible motive power that spins the universe. We pray that a part of this power be apportioned to our needs. Even in our asking, our human deficiencies are filled and we arise strengthened and repaired."

Many a recovered mental patient would say "These words have been proved true in my own experience." Here is how a professional man, who had spent some time in a mental hospital, described his feelings when he had made a complete recovery: "Recovering from mental sickness is a process of reawakening. But in waking up to myself, I find that I am lovingly, hopefully, and joyfully awakening also to my fellow men and to God."

It should be of interest now to read from the pen and thoughts of persons who have been patients in a mental hospital and have recovered, as to the progressive nature of their former illness.

The 12 Stages of Mental Sickness

1. We gave too much importance to ourselves and our feelings.

2. Grew inattentive to God's presence, God's providence and God's will.

3. Let the instinct to please ourselves or others take control of our lives.

4. Surrendered to wrong and harmful feelings in order to relieve tension.

5. Began thinking in isolation from others, following feelings and imagination instead of reason.

6. Neglected the care and control of our bodies.

7. Avoided recognizing our mental decline and shrank from the task of changing.

8. Systematically disguised in our imaginations the real nature of our unhealthy conduct.

9. Became a prey to obsessions, delusions and hallucinations.

10. Practised irrational habits, under elated feelings of irresponsibility or despairing feelings of inability or compulsion.

11. Rejected advice and refused to co-operate with help.

12. Lost all insight into our condition.

Following the example of Alcoholics Anonymous, they have worked out twelve steps of recovery. These are:

The 12 Steps of Recovery

1. We admitted we were mentally sick.
2. Endeavoured to co-operate with help.
3. Surrendered ourselves to the Supreme Healer.
4. Made personal inventory and accepted ourselves.
5. Made moral inventory and cleaned out our hearts.
6. Endured until cured.
7. Strengthened and mastered our bodies.
8. Learned to think by reason rather than by feelings and imagination.
9. Trained our wills to govern our feelings.
10. Took our place in society.
11. Grew daily closer to the source of mental health.
12. Carried the message to other mental sufferers.

A few years ago an article appeared in a prominent Sydney, Australia, newspaper. In it the author, who is a professional man and a former mental patient, told of his experiences in a mental hospital. He followed that with this paragraph setting forth the philosophy of those who had come through victoriously:

To repossess our minds and rebuild our lives we had to learn amid shame, tension and fear, to think humbly and to see things as they really are, to expose our false attitudes, to exorcise immaturity and egocentricity, to adjust ourselves to life's basic demands, to think with reason instead of feelings and imagination, to value the things that really matter and disregard the rest, placing above all the personal values that link our lives to God and to our fellow men; to understand suffering, to endure courageously and patiently while we were changing, and to believe with every fibre of our tormented beings that we were still valuable and that we could once again live and love and be happy.[11]

I have in my files a letter from a woman who has made quite a remarkable recovery from mental illness. She states in detail her feelings when she was in the hospital, the treatment she received, how she reacted to it all, and what happened after her discharge. She made little or no progress toward recovery while in the mental hospital except that the more violent fluctuation of her illness subsided somewhat. Her relatives had no hope of her recovery if she remained where she was, and they arranged for her discharge. Her own family physician entered the case at this point. Her general health was sadly in need of upbuilding and he devoted himself to this. For a time she began to make progress in recovery of her mental health as well. Thereafter, a series of unfortunate happenings occurred in her family, and under the pressure of these adverse events she found it very difficult to stand up to life. It seemed as if all the burdens of life were crowding in upon her. At this point she began to look back to her time in the hospital which she had found so trying and remembered that while there she had been free of all her worries about her husband, her children, her housework, troublesome neighbors, finances. There was nothing to worry her, and from time to time there were dreamy phases in which she had exciting and beautiful visions. This is how she puts it:

I can understand why one wants to stay in a hospital like that. When you have taken more than you can stand nature has a way of releasing you from it all. You go into the world of unreality and at times it looks very beautiful. Now I knew I had to face reality or give up completely and surrender to a lifetime in a mental hospital.

At this point the minister of her parish came to see her. Earlier she had been slow in informing him of her condition because she had a sense of shame about her illness. This time she confided in him to the full. He was given the whole story. He listened sympathetically

[11] *Sydney Morning Herald*, July 12, 1961.

assuring her of God's love and care. Then in prayer he committed her to Christ. That spiritual experience did more for her, she said, than the entire period in the hospital. "It seemed to lift me at once out of my depression. It is hard to express something like this," she writes in the letter, "in any words that you put on paper. I seem to be living on a mountaintop of spiritual experience. It seemed as if Christ himself had come to me personally. His presence has ever since been with me. I feel it now, near me as I write this letter. He is my friend in spite of all my imperfections. The following Sunday when I went to church it seemed as if the glory of God filled the place, and when the service was over I wondered why everyone else had not been aware of this and how they could speak of trifling everyday things."

Some who read this may be inclined to dismiss the experience of this woman as something unreal and probably associated with her mental illness. If so such persons are sadly lacking in an understanding of the variety and power of religious experience. To a limited number of dedicated persons there are given from time to time high moments when God's presence is very real and near. This has been the experience of saints and mystics in every period of Christian history. The genuineness and reality of my correspondent's experience is amply attested by the fact that she has translated it into practical service in Christ's Kingdom. She is now completely adjusted in all her social relations and is very popular with her friends. She is doing constructive and helpful church work, and for a time has been teaching a class of teen-age boys. The closing words in her letter are these: "My faith has brought me through some very heavy 'storms' and I know beyond a shadow of a doubt it will stay with me for the rest of my life until I reach the journey's end."

Here indeed is striking confirmation of what happens when a pastor is alert and brings the resources of religion to bear upon the life of a parishioner. It also indicates the road along which pastors of all religious denominations should travel in leading their people into more enlightened attitudes toward the mentally and emotionally ill.

6

Psychosomatic Illness

IN THE PAST thirty years we have heard a great deal about psycho-somatic medicine. The term "psychosomatic" has now become a part of our everyday speech, and most people have a general under-standing of its meaning. It has come about through a fresh realiza-tion of the interaction and interdependence of psychic (mental) and somatic (bodily) phenomena. One hears psychosomatic medicine frequently referred to as a new development of medical science. Certainly the part it has played in the medical science of the last quarter century is a new emphasis, but for many centuries it has been common knowledge even among nonmedical writers that the illnesses that affect the mind affect the body, too. So we have Lu-cretius, the Roman poet, writing in the first century before Christ:

> For when the body's sick and ill at ease
> The mind doth often share in the disease.

Nathaniel Hawthorne in *The Scarlet Letter*, too, has made a dis-cerning observation: "A bodily disease which we look upon as whole and entire within itself, may, after all, be but a symptom of some ailment of the spiritual part."

The central concern of psychosomatic medicine is with the emo-tions, which, medical authorities assure us, can produce dysfunction in the organs of the body. They may cause overactivity of the voluntary nervous system and the glands of internal secretion. Let us take, for instance, the state of anger or rage. This can be a destructive emotion. Now what effect does it have on the physiological structure of the individual? When one is in a state of rage the blood pressure is definitely raised, the pulse rate is increased, and the respiratory rate is also decidedly increased. If the rage is sustained for some time, definite damage can be done to the organs of the body. Physicians tell us that if the anger passes, then the heightened physical processes begin to subside. If the rage or anger becomes chronic, that is, more or less continuous, then the symptoms described above will persist.

Doctor L. C. Kolb,[1] an eminent authority in the field of psychosomatic medicine, gives a partial list of physical illnesses that may be produced by psychological or emotional stress. Among these are pulmonary tuberculosis, cardiovascular disorders (relating to the heart and blood vessels), respiratory ailments (such as asthma, etc.), gastrointestinal upsets, migraine and tension headaches, disturbed diabetic metabolism, Parkinson's disease, gastric and duodenal ulcers, etc. He flatly asserts that emotional problems aggravate all illnesses and the denial of the existence of such emotional disturbances provokes still greater distress in the patient. Most impressive is the way he points out the concern of experts in this field with the situation that produces distress and the thoughts that precipitate personality disturbances. While, as we have indicated earlier, the concept of the psychosomatic is not new, yet the emphasis on the fact that even the thoughts that we think can be producers of physical illness is something that this century has brought to the fore. All thoroughly qualified physicians now take into account unfailingly the psychosomatic elements in any illness.

Undoubtedly, one of the greatest authorities of our time on the

[1] Professor and Chairman of the Department of Psychiatry, College of Physicians and Surgeons, Columbia University.

subject of psychosomatic illnesses is Dr. Hans Selye. Some of his new concepts on mental and physical illness are explained in his book entitled *The Stress of Life*. In a chapter on "Psychosomatic Implications," Dr. Selye deals with the manifold interactions between somatic and psychic reactions. He compares the effect on a person who is keyed up with emotional tension to the process of raising the key of a violin by tightening the strings. At times this may be quite appropriate and could assist our endeavors. When, however, too much tension has been generated it infallibly will interfere with our effectiveness.

Dr. Selye has some helpful suggestions on getting rid of worrisome thoughts. He reminds us that we cannot by an act of will dismiss anxieties. If it is impossible to eliminate their cause we must find something constructive to put in their place so that the new impulse of a higher order will expel the distructive worries. "Nothing" he says "erases unpleasant thoughts more effectively than conscious concentration on pleasant ones."

As for the matter of sleep, he strongly urges that we try to confine our most intense activity to the earlier hours of the day. Later we should ensure that the work is as near as possible to completion. No loose tag-ends should remain at the end of the day. If we leave too many tasks uncompleted we are storing up "self-maintaining tensions" that are going to keep us awake at night. For my own part, I have found it worthwhile to get up, even in the middle of the night, and write letters, grapple with an unsolved problem, or do whatever else should be necessary to complete a transaction that has become a source of worry, thus getting it off my mind.

Dr. Selye recommends that if we have, for one reason or another, been compelled to cut down on our sleep at night we should snatch an opportunity in the course of the day to have a nap in order to replenish our resources. A brief afternoon rest or sleep is highly advised by competent medical men. Many people, including Winston Churchill, have found this procedure to be practical and of great value.

The importance of psychosomatic considerations is seen in case histories found in medical writings. One such is a chapter by Dr. Jerome Hartz in *Personality, Stress and Tuberculosis*.[2] Dr. Hartz devotes eight and a half pages to the case of a young woman whose disturbed emotions prevented for many months any possibility of her being healed of tuberculosis. He describes in detail the kind of life-and-death struggle that was going on within the personality of his patient. Unless some resolution of this conflict could be found the outcome of her illness might well be fatal. At thirty years of age her life was dominated by the fear that latent pulmonary tuberculosis would flare up violently. She was a biologist by training and a person of considerable ability but could make little progress in her studies because of all her anxieties concerning her health, the people around her, and life's responsibilities in general. She contracted a mild case of tuberculosis when she was twenty-seven years old and just at the beginning of her postgraduate work. Seven or eight months in a sanitarium started her on the way to recovery. After she had spent a month or two at home convalescing she had a severe relapse. Her mother had made very heavy emotional demands on her, which she was unable to satisfy, and had accused her of being too cold, too remote, too unfeeling. At the same time the mother prided herself on her kindness to the girl and her great care of her. It became apparent to the young woman that beneath the friendly protestations of her mother there was latent and definite hostility. The patient's progress toward recovery was slow and there were intermittent periods of retrogression.

Earlier in life when she first went to college she had contracted a marriage with a young man. She was only nineteen at the time. The marriage lasted only a few months and then a friendship with a college girl fared little better. She was worn out trying to meet the pace of life at college and to establish a friendship that would last. Finally, she gave up the struggle and saw in illness a perfect escape. And so, eventually, she was taken to a sanitarium. Dr. Hartz suggests that the retreat to the silence of the mountains and the indo-

[2] Edited by T. J. Sparer (New York: International Universities Press, 1956).

lence of bedrest with solicitous attention from the nurses meant to
her a return to infancy. She luxuriated in the anticipation of doing
nothing—free of guilt about it because she was ill and nothing could
be expected of her.

Trouble rose again when the mother began to visit her daughter.
Tension mounted. Even though the patient was living in a sanitarium, the mother prepared to stay with her for several weeks. The
patient knew that in this time her mother would take complete
charge of her life, tell her what friends to cast aside and what she
was to do with every moment of her time. Little by little she developed an intense hatred of her mother, and that hatred turned in upon
herself with destructive results. However, with the stanch help of the
doctor, she decided to live her own life, and so informed her mother.
The mother, sensing her determination, gave up the struggle to control her. Thereafter, tuberculosis no longer seemed a friendly refuge
and the sanitarium no longer an escape where she might be babied
and taken care of without embarrassment and shame. Now she
began to make excellent progress. With the change in her attitude to
her mother and the fact that she learned to exteriorize the hatred she
had felt toward her and ultimately to master it, the patient's whole
attitude toward the pulmonary tuberculosis changed. She was now
well on the road to eventual recovery. Nothing whatsoever is said by
Dr. Hartz about the religious attitude of the young woman, but a
renewed faith is implicit in the total situation. In the doctor's attitude there was great understanding and kindliness.

I have given this case history in detail because it underlines the
powerful effect of emotions on the health and general well-being of a
patient. I am convinced that a much earlier recovery could have
been made if this young woman had received spiritual counsel and
therapy.

Dr. Bernard Martin, a Swiss pastor and psychiatrist, has much to
say about the widespread ramifications of the psychosomatic. He
quotes Dr. P. Granjon, surgeon and professor in the Faculty of
Medicine at Marseille, France:

For a long time now we have recognized the repercussions of mental factors on health: we say of one person that he is "torn by remorse," or another that he is "eaten up with jealousy," but never before the recent developments of psychosomatic medicine would one have dared to link the onset of pulmonary tuberculosis with a sentimental disappointment, making the one responsible for the other.[3]

Dr. Granjon then notes a number of the physical illnesses that can be directly traced to psychosomatic influences and he concludes with these words: "One of my teachers, although he was a very rationalistic surgeon, was forced to note how often a cancer of the breast followed close on a great sorrow, heartrending and sickening, such as can follow the death of a child."[4]

I have described a number of illnesses which medical authors attribute to harmful emotional states. To some people this may seem a very depressing picture. To me it is quite the contrary. I rejoice in this very close relationship of body and mind. If destructive emotions are capable of producing illnesses that have in them the potentiality of pain and death, by the same token good emotions are powerful factors working for health and human well-being.

We have just seen what unstable and unhealthy emotions did in provoking illness and impending recovery. Let us now look at the opposite side of the coin and see what a radiant faith and disciplined emotions did for a victim of the same illness as in the first instance —tuberculosis.

The subject of this case history is a businessman, forty-five years of age, who was deeply and truly Christian in all his relationships. Quite unknown to him since his boyhood he had carried within himself the seeds of pulmonary tuberculosis. A simple cold developed into an upper respiratory illness and very quickly into tuberculosis. He went to a clinic and was told that he would have to give up his business for approximately one year. All control of it would have to be turned over to others; they would bear the responsibilities

[3] *Healing for You* (Richmond: John Knox Press, 1965), p. 63.
[4] *Ibid.*, p. 64.

and worries. No matter what the results were in his business he had to be prepared to accept the consequences. Very quickly he put his business in the hands of a trusted assistant. He committed his life, his loved ones, and indeed, all his affairs into the hands of God, and went to a sanitarium. All his thought and energy he now put into the business of getting well. Obeying to the letter all instructions given him by the attendant physician, he followed strictly the diet, periods of rest, and moderate exercise prescribed. In his daily devotions he thanked God for his increasing strength and for the hope of complete recovery. Shortly he became a source of comfort and good cheer to all the patients. He organized various social activities to get them acquainted with each other and used his influence as a businessman to get hundreds of additional books for the library. He was the center of radiant good cheer. He came out of the sanitarium completely recovered. Under medical advice he began to work a few hours a day. Before long he resumed his full schedule of work. Afterward, as he talked to friends about his experience in the hospital, he said, "Whenever any negative or disturbing thoughts came to me, before they had a chance to get in their ugly work of depression, I would turn my thoughts to God and to His care of His trustful children. I invariably kept the morning watch with my Bible. The presence of Christ beside me became very real, and in my judgment, all this was a meaningful factor in my getting well." Here we see emotions which might have become disturbing and destructive, employed for beneficent results.

The New Testament is a valuable document warranted to produce that inner peace, that spirit of hopefulness, that faith and love, all of which are mighty factors in human well-being. If it be true, as the ablest medical experts say, that the thoughts we think, the ideals we espouse, the emotions that dominate us, can be for each of us a blessing or a bane, then we should resolutely seek the guidance of Him who is "the way, the truth and the life." In Paul's Letter to the Philippians there is set forth a Christian "Magna Charta" of healthy-mindedness, a prescription for good health and radiant living:

Don't worry over anything whatever; tell God every detail of your needs in earnest and thankful prayer, and the peace of God, which transcends human understanding, will keep constant guard over your hearts and minds as they rest in Christ Jesus.

Here is a last piece of advice. If you believe in goodness and if you value the approval of God, fix your minds on whatever is true and honourable and just and pure and lovely and praiseworthy. Model your conduct on what you have learned from me, on what I have told you and shown you, and you will find that the God of peace will be with you (4:6-9, PHILLIPS).

This passage from Philippians, incidentally, was a favorite of the businessman mentioned a moment ago. The various factors that played a part in his recovery are worth noting: First, he had full confidence in the medical knowledge and skill of the superintendent of the sanitarium. Second, he achieved a disciplined acceptance of the treatment outlined for him and the imposed daily routine. Third, he had a firm conviction that he was going to get well, while at the same time trusting God for the outcome and maintaining daily fellowship with Him. Fourth, he believed that the prayers of his loved ones and of certain groups in the home church, offered in his behalf, were helping to bring him increased strength and physical and mental well-being. A year or two later at a conference I met the superintendent of the sanitarium. He said that the faith and courage of my friend and his undaunted hopefulness did more toward his recovery than the medication and treatment which he had received. Sir William Osler, one of the greatest of all medical teachers, reminded his students that the fate of tubercular patients depended more on what they had in their heads and in their hearts than what was in their chests.

Dr. Russell L. Dicks, who has shed so much light on the opportunities afforded for a pastoral ministry in the sickroom, never ceased to interest himself in the relation between the mind and spirit of man and his body. On one occasion he wrote that only seventeen out of every hundred patients passing through the outpatient department of Mayo Clinic are suffering from organic diseases. Approximately the same percentage of psychosomatic patients, we are told, is found in other well-known hospitals. It is an open question how accurate these percentages are, but certainly the number of patients with psychosomatic illness in hospitals all across the land must run according to available statistics from 60 to 80 per cent. "What of these nonorganic cases?" Russell Dicks asks, and answers his own question: "Too often they are given reassurance that does not reassure, hope that does not give hope, and often there is a lack of investigation of the psychic factors in the situation."

Many of the symptoms suffered by psychosomatic patients are due to an attempt on their part to escape from reality. They are unable to come to grips with the problems that face them on every hand. Persons accustomed to dealing with the sick have often commented on the fact that an important consideration in illness is the sense of isolation which hospital patients feel because of their separation from society. It is something like the loneliness that overtakes many soldiers in military hospitals.

Both pastors and people frequently assume that the visitation of the sick is a development that belongs to more recent years. It may come as quite a surprise to know that the greatly beloved clergyman Richard Baxter of England, in the middle of the seventeenth century, took extraordinary care of the eight hundred families in his charge. He made an effort to visit each of these families once a year. It is hard for us nowadays even with all our modes of transportation to conceive how he ever could have accomplished this. It was his conviction that a word in season spoken to an individual may be used of God more effectively than many sermons. Said he, in his book *The Reformed Pastor*, "A minister is not merely to be a public preacher, but to be known as a counselor for their souls as the physician is for their bodies and the lawyer for their estates."[5]

Martin Luther, too, exercised an extraordinary ministry to the sick. He made no apologies for visiting the sickroom and considered that his presence there was as important as that of the physician. He also was perfectly well aware of what we now call psychosomatic

[5] New York: American Tract Society, n.d., p. 152.

illnesses. He was convinced that many diseases have their origin in morbid spiritual conditions. On one occasion he remarked: "When the heart is troubled and sorrowful, there follows also weakness of the body."

Luther on a memorable occasion found himself face to face with the serious illness of one of his dearest friends and colleagues, Philip Melanchthon. It is worth noting that in Melanchthon's illness there was a definite psychosomatic element. Both Melanchthon and Luther had been involved in a bigamous marriage question. Philip Melanchthon was a man of a very sensitive conscience—a delicate and gentle man. His biographers tell us that he became despondent over what he regarded as his own involvement in an unethical decision and became ill. His condition grew steadily worse until his life was despaired of. When Luther reached his friend he was shocked to see that Melanchthon had all the appearances of a dying man. His eyes were sunken in his head. He could no longer speak and he showed no signs of being able to hear. Most of the time he appeared unconscious. For many hours now he had recognized no one, and on his face was the pallor of death. Luther went over to the window of the bedroom, and kneeling there, prayed with great fervor—the fervor of an unquenchable faith. The Reformer became assured that God had given him an affirmative answer. Rising from his knees, he went back to the bed, and taking Melanchthon by the hand, said to him in a strong, clear voice: "Be of good cheer, Philip, thou shalt not die." Luther's words reached down into the very deeps of Melanchthon's personality—down beneath the barriers that weakness and the approach of death had erected. His words struck an answering chord in the heart of his friend. Where the best efforts of the doctors had failed, spiritual power succeeded.

It is not difficult for anyone who has visited often with the sick, and who has seen persons in a coma come back to consciousness while prayer was being offered, to visualize this scene. I have myself witnessed this happening many times and always it is an unforgettable experience. Melanchthon slowly returned to consciousness and became aware of his friend's presence. Doubtless he heard his words. Luther prevailed on Melanchthon to take some nourishment. Little by little his strength began to return. When he opened his eyes and looked at the wall at the foot of his bed, he saw in the bold handwriting of Martin Luther, these words from Psalm 118 (vs. 17): "I shall not die, but live, and declare the works of the Lord." And live he did, to carry on nobly the work of the Reformation for fourteen years after Luther himself had been called home to God.

James Dale Van Buskirk,[6] who is both a medical doctor and a minister, tells of a case history set forth by Dr. Alvarez. A woman came to him for help. It appears that during the financial crisis of 1931 her father had used up all her money to stop a run on his bank. He lost everything. She became so angry about the loss of her fortune that she went to her father and gave him a severe tongue-lashing. The father said nothing in reply, but went into his room and shot himself in the head. He left a note saying that he was repaying the money in the only way he could, with his life insurance. The woman had a breakdown—nervously and physically. She was overwhelmed with a sense of guilt for her father's death. Dr. Alvarez, in this case history, adds: "Naturally, there wasn't much that I could do to help her."[7]

This episode narrated by one physician, who is probably a psychiatrist, and commented on by another, is a startling illustration of the inadequacy of unaided secular therapy to come to grips with some of the most soul-shattering of human problems. Here was a situation that cried aloud for spiritual help. Nobody who has witnessed the power of faith in God to transform desperate life situations would ever be guilty of writing this sentence: "Naturally, there wasn't much that I could do to help her."

Every experienced and dedicated Christian counselor knows that when all other resources fail the Great Physician is "able to save them to the uttermost that come unto God by him" (Heb. 7:25).

[6] *Religion, Healing and Health* (New York: Macmillan Company, 1952), p. 97.
[7] Dr. Walter C. Alvarez, *Nervousness, Indigestion, and Pain* (New York: Paul B. Hoeber, n.d.), p. 286.

It is quite evident that our Lord was acquainted with this psychosomatic phenomenon, though not, of course, with the technical details now asociated with it. In at least two instances (Mark 2:1-12, John 5:1-9) in His ministry He traced a physical malady back to a moral malady, the disease of the body to an illness of the spirit. As we might expect, Shakespeare also refers to the relations between mind and body. In *King Lear*[8] he writes:

> We are not ourselves
> when nature, being oppress'd, commands the mind
> to suffer with the body.

Oftentimes the key to some illness, mental or physical, in the adult will be found in the early experiences of childhood. Wordsworth, in his poem, "My Heart Leaps Up" says: "The Child is father of the Man." Those words have a depth and significance of which Wordsworth could scarcely have dreamed, for the maladies of adulthood often have their roots deep within childhood. Freud used to say that much of the suffering in adults comes from the memories, conscious and unconscious, of childhood. If one delves into the roots of many a disorder of later years, he will find that they go deep into the problems and tragic experiences of childhood. Psychosomatic medicine recognizes that the character and personality of the patient are as important as the character of his illness. It concerns itself with the patient as a person; his total organism is regarded as important as his organ pathology. The individual's background from childhood, his qualities as a person, and his characteristic attitudes to life will all be a part of the dynamic interplay within the person. It has been well said: "Psychosomatic medicine seeks to promote the total understanding, the total treatment and the total well-being of patients."[9]

Psychosomatic medicine has much to offer for the study of pastors and seminary teachers. Whatever may have been the recognition in earlier years of the human mind and body, certainly in the last half-

[8] Act II, Scene 4.
[9] *Personality, Stress and Tuberculosis*, edited by T. J. Sparer.

century prior to this new development, teachers in medical schools
had little to say about the effect of the mind on the body. I heard Dr.
Earl D. Bond, formerly head of the Psychiatric Department of the
University of Pennsylvania, in an address to doctors and ministers
say: "When I was beginning my medical studies a half a century ago
the surgeon in chief in his opening remarks to the class of young
medical students, said, 'May I point out to you that man has a soul
and a body. Now, that's enough for the soul. For the next four years
you'll hear all about his body.' "

This lecturer on surgery was not alone in holding such a materialistic viewpoint. The mind of man suffered as much neglect in
anatomical studies as did the soul. Dr. G. Canby Robinson of Johns
Hopkins Hospital, Baltimore, addressing a public meeting in the
Academy of Medicine, asserted: "Man is a unity of mind and body.
Medicine must consider this unity. Physiology, chemistry and biology cannot alone be dealt with separately; they form two phases of a
single problem."

Dr. Flanders Dunbar of the Presbyterian Medical Center, New
York, presents a dramatic instance of the complications produced by
human emotions on the course of a physical illness.[10] Dr. Dunbar
tells of the case history of a diabetic in Presbyterian Hospital. The
patient had been making good progress. It looked as though he
might soon be discharged. Then one day his blood sugar rose alarm-
ingly without any change whatsoever in his diet, medication, or general routine. A consultation was held but no adequate explanation
was forthcoming, until a nurse inquired whether it might be possible
that a letter received by the patient a day or so before could account
for the change in his condition. On inquiry, it was found that in the
letter the patient had been told that his corporation planned shortly
to retire him. The disturbing emotions aroused by this bad news
arrested his progress and actually reversed his condition. Someone
remarked that it was astonishing that the power of an emotion could

---

[10] *"Mind and Body: Psychosomatic Medicine* (New York: Random House,
1947), p. 198.

be measured in terms so tangible as some grains of sugar. Dr. Dunbar put it graphically, remarking that disturbing thoughts had "changed the chemistry of the patient's blood."

Every pastor who is engaged in counseling knows how powerfully the principle of psychosomatic influences can work in the life of the sick, whether of mind or of body. The person who has achieved wholeness in his spiritual life, with no gnawing anxieties distressing him, has a far better chance for total well-being. Every Christian minister should remember and never dare to forget that he is an ambassador of Christ. The Great Physician has entrusted him with a ministry to the spirit of man and indirectly also to the mind and body. This type of ministry of necessity goes beyond the practice of the psychiatrist or the physician. Christ said that he had come to make men whole. This, too, should be central in our ministry to men and women. The minister in his counseling will employ what we have every right to call spiritual therapy. It exerts a healing influence, as we have seen, on mind and body. Spiritual therapy can penetrate the deepest recesses of the human personality.

A striking tribute was paid to a spiritual ministry by a notable physician whose writings I have previously quoted, Dr. G. Canby Robinson of Johns Hopkins Hospital, University, and Medical School.

In an address at the Academy of Medicine in New York, Dr. Robinson told of a case history of a man who came to the Johns Hopkins clinic complaining of a heart condition. Said Dr. Robinson, "We gave him a thoroughgoing examination: electrocardiograph, X rays, etc., and discovered that his heart had been seriously injured. The prognosis was not good. We instructed him to give up his work, which was plumbing, and take an eight months' complete rest. He was to avoid all exertion. If he followed these instructions, we intimated that he could add some years to his life. On his records it was noted, however, that he would be doomed to semi-invalidism." Some months later a caseworker at the clinic had been going over the records of patients, when she came upon the medical history of this heart-case. She wondered what had happened to this man, so journeyed to his home to find out. His wife told the caseworker that her husband was back at work and had been working for some months. "When she reported this to the clinic," said Dr. Robinson, "we asked the man to come in for another complete examination. He looked the picture of health. He reported that he had started working a couple of hours a day but lived within careful bounds and had given up several of the disorderly habits he had previously practiced. He told us that after his visit to the clinic he had been resting around home for a month or two. Becoming wearied of idleness and looking for reading matter, he came upon a Bible and began to read it. He said that it had a profound effect on his life, indeed altered his whole mode of thinking and living. He became a Christian and attended a nearby church. When he returned to the clinic we proceeded to examine him with the electrocardiograph, X rays, and direct stethoscopic examination. We could find no trace of the illness which he had suffered a little over one year before."

There is nothing to surprise any active pastor-counselor in this testimony. The unusual feature is that it should have come from a well-known medical author. Unfortunately, there has oftentimes been a breakdown of communication between two important disciplines, psychiatry and religion. When this happens we hear the words spoken by those who are working in another discipline, but we fail to understand them. We read what they have written but fail to comprehend the meaning of their presentation. Consequently, on both sides there is sometimes misunderstanding and antagonism. It has oftentimes been said that the two disciplines to which I have referred are separated by a chasm that is unbridgeable. Theology, it is said, is primarily concerned with God. Psychology and psychiatry are primarily concerned with man. But to say this is to overlook the fact that on the functional level there is a branch of theology called Pastoral Theology in which man is decidedly an object of interest and concern. So, on the practical or operational level, psychology and theology have much to say to each other, and on many occasions one interpenetrates the other. In practice, at times there is a definite overlapping.

William B. Terhune, M.D., who served for so many years as medical superintendent of Silver Hill, Connecticut, suggests that the goal of the psychiatrist is "the rehabilitation of the total personality." A clergyman quoting this statement added, "The total personality of man certainly includes his spirituality so that using another discipline and by a different approach we, too, seek the redemption of human personality and our function is as valid as is that of the psychiatrist or the physician."[11]

In many cases of psychosomatic illness it has even been found that after all the required medical therapy has been applied in a given case, the psychosomatic patient returns again with the old malady or perhaps with a new one. Professor Gordon W. Allport has suggested that in all matters of health and wholeness a "unifying philosophy of life" has very high value for personal adjustment. We are all familiar with Dr. Jung's comment years ago when he affirmed that a belief-system was an essential ingredient to the recovery of his patients, especially when they had attained middle age. Oftentimes the patient comes to the hospital burdened with a crushing sense of real guilt or a feeling of the meaninglessness of existence. These are prominent factors in inducing illness, and if they are not dealt with when physical therapies are applied in the hospital, the chances of an improvement are not encouraging.

A series of articles appeared recently in medical journals dealing with the destructive aspects of a sense of guilt. Dr. David Delgun of the School of Religion, University of Iowa, has suggested that many psychosomatic symptoms may well be the "amplified and distorted voice of conscience." In most cases of neurotic guilt, which has no basis in reality, it will take the skillful ministry of a psychiatrist to unravel the tangled strands of this malady. But when it comes to real guilt, from actual moral transgression, generally the pastor alone, ministering to the distressed person in the name of Christ, through the teachings and the insights of the Christian faith, can bring to a troubled soul the assurances of divine forgiveness and spiritual re-

---

[11] From an address delivered at Silver Hill. J.S.B.

newal. Truly, both medicine and religion have much to say to each other and only as they work together in the spirit of dedication seeking to restore wholeness to distressed souls can they fulfill their responsibility to the human personalities entrusted to their care.

7

The Limitless Resources of Faith

"Faith" is one of the meaningful words of our language. It has a secular as well as a spiritual connotation. Faith may have reference to a bond of fidelity, to an agreement, to a trust. We speak of a person as a man of faith, and of our faith in a promise made to us. We also have faith in certain persons and speak of "keeping the faith." In a more spiritual sense we discuss faith in God, faith in the authority of the Bible, faith in the creeds and doctrines of the Church. In specific areas the two meanings, secular and spiritual, blend together. Dr. Karl Menninger says, "Faith in something is a sine qua non of sentient life."[1] He is referring to faith in such things as a set of values, a philosophy, a person. He takes note of the fact that faith plays a vital role in the practice of medicine whether it be as physician, surgeon, psychiatrist, or other form of service. A doctor's success or failure in dealing with a sick person may depend, Dr. Menninger suggests, on whether or not he secures and maintains the faith of the patient in himself and in his power to help.

Similar thoughts with respect to the place of faith in the practice of medicine were set forth by Sir William Osler, the world-renowned physician. He lived at a time when little or nothing was heard of psychosomatic medicine, yet in all his practice he never failed to

[1] *"The Vital Balance"* (New York: Viking Press, 1963), p. 374.

stress the influence exerted by the mind on the body and the body on the mind. Dr. Harvey W. Cushing, eminent neurologist of Boston, has recorded in his biography of Osler some of the physician's reflections on this subject. Sir William had delivered an address that attracted wide attention in Britain. It was entitled, "The Faith That Heals." Here are some of Osler's words:

> Nothing in life is more wonderful than faith, the one great moving force which we can neither weigh in the balance nor test in the crucible. . . . To each one of the religions, past or present, faith has been the Jacob's ladder. Creeds pass; an inexhaustible supply of faith remains with which man proceeds to rebuild the temples, churches, chapels and shrines. . . . Christendom lives on it, and countless thousands are happy in the possession of that most touching of all confessions, Lord I believe; help thou my unbelief.[2]

In this paper Osler tells of a ten-year-old girl who lay paralyzed in a New Jersey town. Her relatives and family were worn out constantly serving her. When Dr. Osler was called in on the case he changed the entire routine, put the young girl in a hospital and, sensing a neurotic element in the situation, assured her of recovery. The girl's pleasant surroundings and a few simple measures of medical attention brought positive results. Within a fortnight she was on her feet and walking around the hospital square. Her recovery was complete. He anticipated psychosomatic medicine. The subject of the relation of the mind to the body, said Dr. Osler, was of great interest to him. The author of the biography himself, Dr. Cushing, adds: "Faith has always been an essential factor in the practice of medicine."

A considerable number of religious movements have grown up in Western civilization in the last half-century based in part on the influence of mind on body. Some of these are New Thought, Unity, Four-Square Gospel, Christian Science, Pentecostal groups, Spiritualist churches, etc. All of these in one form or another have

[2] Quoted in Cushing, *Life of Sir William Osler* (New York: Oxford University Press, 1940), pp. 908-9.

engaged in "faith healing." It is not my intention to write critically of these movements even though at times they have set back the cause of spiritual healing by extremist measures and a deliberate flaunting of the findings of medical science. First, because there is no doubt that in the case of each of these some good has been accomplished. It is true that oftentimes extravagant claims are made with no medical diagnosis either before or after the "healing." Nevertheless, these movements would not have persisted were it not for the "sound wood that keeps them floating." Faith is so powerful a force that it sometimes produces results in the most unpromising situations. The second reason why I shall not deal critically with these healing cults is because they have at least made an attempt to fulfill the commandment of Christ when he charged his followers to go forth to preach and heal. It ill behooves the historic Christian churches, which oftentimes have fallen down so badly in this whole matter of a ministry to the sick, to cast aspersions at those who at least have tried to do their best. Anyone interested in a critical analysis of modern faith-healing cults will find this in *Faith Healing and the Christian Faith.*[3]

When I suggested that at times good may be accomplished by some of the healing cults referred to, this should not be taken as an approval of the particular doctrines espoused by these bodies. Any success that may be achieved in healing need have no relation whatsoever to the teachings they proclaim.

It should be said at this point that there is no evidence in the Gospel records that our Lord regarded His ministry to the sick as the main emphasis of His mission among men. On more than one occasion He turned aside from the healing ministry that He might engage more directly in proclaiming the Kingdom of God and man's need of reconciliation with his Heavenly Father. When the crowd at Capernaum endeavored to compel Him to continue His ministry of healing, Jesus said, "I must preach the Kingdom of God to other cities also: *for therefore am I sent*" (Luke 4:43). It was physically

---

[3] Wade H. Boggs, Jr. (Richmond: John Knox Press, 1956).

impossible for Jesus to deal with more than the merest fraction of the sick in Judah and Galilee. Tens of thousands remained unhealed. When our Lord healed the impotent man at the Pool of Bethesda, He left scores of others unhealed in that desolate and depressing place. Even in His actual healings He was not primarily concerned with healing the ills of the human body, but sought in every instance the redemption of the whole personality.

In the ministry of our Lord a primary place was given to the spiritual force known as "faith." The word "faith" occurs scores of times in the New Testament. Here are a few of our Lord's own references to faith: "O ye of little faith" (Matt. 6:30). "I have not found so great faith, no not in Israel" (Matt. 8:10). "If ye have faith as a grain of mustard seed, ye shall say unto this mountain, Remove hence to yonder place; and it shall remove; and nothing shall be impossible unto you" (Matt. 17:20). "And he said unto them, how is it that ye have no faith?" (Mark 4:40). "Jesus saith unto them, have faith in God" (Mark 11:22). The fact that His words at this point did not fall on deaf ears is revealed by the disciples' request: "Lord, increase our faith" (Luke 17:5).

Time and again we see our Lord encouraging the faith of the sick; urging them to look for and gratefully receive God's gift of healing (Matt., chs. 8-9). He always welcomed every evidence of faith on the part of those who journeyed with Him and tried to convey to them something of that glow of confident optimism and power which was unfailingly manifested in His own ministry. Matthew tells us that two blind men followed Jesus, crying, "Thou Son of David, have mercy on us." When they approached Him, He said, "Believe ye that I am able to do this? They said unto him, Yea Lord. Then touched he their eyes saying, According to your faith be it unto you." Their sight was restored as a definite reward of their faith. To the woman who felt that if she could but touch His garment she would be healed, Jesus said, "Daughter, be of good comfort; thy faith hath made thee whole." Again when four friends brought a man sick of the palsy and laid him at the feet of Jesus, Matthew tells us that it was the evidence of the friends' faith in what Jesus could do for him that brought to the invalid both healing and forgiveness. Once more, when He restored the servant of a Roman Centurion He told his master, "Go thy way; and as thou hast believed, so be it done unto thee. And his servant was healed in the selfsame hour." All of these episodes are reported in two chapters of Matthew's Gospel.

What is this remarkable spiritual power that brought such blessings to people? Jesus called it faith. Faith, according to Jesus, is not primarily intellectual assent to a theological proposition. Neither is it evidence presented in support of truth. Our Lord's view of faith is that it must always contain an element of personal confidence, self-commitment, and trust. Faith is an experience of fellowship with Christ wherein we find moral and spiritual unity with Him. By faith God offers us a gift and we receive it. William James gives a helpful definition of faith. "Faith means belief in something concerning which doubt is still theoretically possible; and the test of belief is willingness to act in a cause the prosperous issue of which is not certified to us in advance."[4] The "willingness to act" referred to by James is that commitment, that yielding of ourselves, that surrender we make to Christ. To illustrate what he means by faith, James suggests the plight of a man on a mountainside who finds his pathway blocked. Only one way of escape remains—a leap across a crevasse. The mountain-climber knows that he will not succeed in the leap unless he has every confidence that it can be made successfully. He also knows that failure will mean death. Faith that the leap can be successfully made will contribute to the desired result. So, says James, the future is conditioned by your faith. Thus "faith creates its own verification. Believe what you desire for the belief is one of the indispensable preliminary conditions of the realization of its object." Faith therefore involves the willingness to take a risk, willingness to venture our all on the hope of success.

William James's definition of faith as commitment or surrender is taken up by Paul Tillich:

[4] The Will to Believe and Other Essays in Popular Philosophy (New York: Longmans, Green, 1904), p. 90.

. . . faith means being grasped by a power that is greater than we are, a power that shakes us and turns us, and transforms us and heals us. Surrender to this power is faith. The people whom Jesus could heal and can heal are those who did and do this self-surrender to the healing power in Him. They surrendered their persons, split, contradicting themselves, disgusted and despairing about themselves, hateful of themselves, and therefore hostile towards everybody else; afraid of life, burdened with guilt feelings, accusing and excusing themselves, fleeing from others into loneliness, fleeing from themselves to others, trying finally to escape from the threats of existence into the painful and deceptive safety of mental and bodily disease. As such beings they surrendered to Jesus and this surrender is what we call faith.[5]

This mighty spiritual force known as faith our Lord committed to his followers. It had healed and transformed each of them and they knew that they had been entrusted with a moral and spiritual dynamic that possessed sufficient power to conquer the far-flung Roman empire and bring it as a trophy to lay at the feet of their crucified but risen Lord.

No man or woman is prepared for a mission of Christian healing who has not experienced this power and is not prepared to channel it into other lives. Let us look at a case history of present-day healing. It is concerned with an American businessman who rose to a place of leadership in an organization that is known in the United States from coast to coast and indeed in all parts of the world. He has traveled through practically every state in the Union, all provinces in Canada, and in many other lands. For a year or two he was a professor in Columbia University's School of Journalism. In this post he found the work a heavy strain. He had given all that he had to business-travel and research and various forms of national and international activities for thirty-six years.

In the year 1958, during the summer, this man took a trip to the Mediterranean for rest and refreshment. Returning to work he discovered that he was still tired. While in a depressed state of mind he suffered an attack of virus influenza. The symptoms were high tem-

---

[5] "On Healing" by Paul Tillich, in *Pastoral Psychology* (June, 1955), p. 28.

perature and extreme fatigue. Later while in Canton, Ohio watching a television program he observed a blur in his right eye. He made an appointment with his eye doctor and when he was asked to read a diagram on the wall he failed miserably in the test. The physician said that the virus had hit the optic nerve and had done destructive work. "Go home," said the doctor "and see your own physician. I will give you a note that you can hand him when you get there."

En route to his home the man opened the note and found that the doctor who had examined him suggested to his own physician that the patient should be tested carefully for the possibility of a brain tumor. His doctor put him in a hospital where he was examined several times by ophthalmologists, neurologists, etc. The diagnosis was retro-bulbar-neuritis with a withering of a considerable portion of the eye nerve. Ten per cent of the sight had gone from the right eye, 50 per cent from the left, and the indications were that there would be further deterioration. He was sent to St. Luke's Hospital in New York City for further observation and from there was referred to the Presbyterian Medical Center, the Department of Ophthalmology, in New York. After a consultation there with several doctors he was given the same verdict: no hope of improvement of his sight and real danger of further deterioration.

He kept going the rounds of the doctors and hospitals. At Duke University the diagnosis was identical with the former one and the doctor added, rather mysteriously, "Some important lines are down in your eyes," referring of course to the nerves. A strong feeling was building up in this man that the deterioration was progressive and that blindness would be his fate. "I was in a constant state of fear, bordering on complete panic," he says. He began to think that the doctors were withholding the truth and that blindness was inevitable. At this point he sought an interview with me at the Fifth Avenue Presbyterian Church. I shall let this man tell his own story in writing:

After I'd poured out my story in full you offered a prayer that moved me deeply—a prayer for God's presence and his healing power. You laid your hands on my head and touched my eyes lightly with your fingers, as you prayed. During that interview, for the first time in my life, I felt a tremendous sense of God's presence and power. It seemed as if a new lease of life had come to me, a feeling of reassurance and inner certainty. You prayed that God's healing power might flow into my mind and body and spirit, and I believe that is exactly what happened. I was delivered from the terrible wilderness of fear and hopelessness.

Recently this man came to see me again, as he has done through the years from time to time. He said: "Can you believe it? The date of that first visit was December 1958, and now I am enjoying the good health that I have had ever since coming to you almost ten years ago. While my eyesight was somewhat deficient during all these years, this fact interfered in no way with my business life or my enjoyment of life in general. Best of all I have never lost faith in God's constant presence and guidance."

The key to the change that occurred in this man was the fact that he had faith—faith in God and in the possibility of healing, and that he surrendered himself wholly to God. When he grasped the reality of God's healing power and committed himself completely to it, his life was transformed. Suddenly he was delivered from paralyzing fear, no longer living in dread as to what the next day might bring. A flood of new energy coursed through his body. Disturbing mental and physical symptoms vanished. His faith was immeasurably strengthened. Prayer became a living reality for him. The future was now bright with hope. He went back to his important and exacting duties and performed them efficiently right up to the time of his retirement a matter of months ago. Now he is rejoicing in having more time than ever before for the duties of Christian citizenship.

Some people find it difficult to accept the fact that faith can transform a human life and bring hope even to the despairing. Physicians too at times find it hard to accept the evidence for spiritual healing with or without medical intervention. Leaders in medical science are fully cognizant of this difficulty.

Dr. Karl Menninger writes:

The reported recovery from such conditions as optic atrophy, epilepsy, feeblemindedness, carcinoma, and advanced mental deterioration evokes curious emotional reactions in doctors, associated with tacit incredulity. We simply cannot quite concede the possibility that immutable laws can be broken. It almost angers a scientific man to be told that a colleague has observed an instance of something contrary to all established medical principles and precedent and pathology. Most of us are like the priest who allegedly refused to look through Galileo's telescope lest, as he said, it destroy his faith.[6]

One ought to be very sympathetic with physicians at this point because on all sides they are pressed to accept wishful thinking for hard medical facts. It must also seem to them as though such happenings are a contradiction of everything that they have studied in medical schools and seen in practice. Nevertheless, such happenings do occur and nobody knows that better than the pastor-counselor who is actively engaged in helping people and in working in close cooperation with physicians.

As I have suggested elsewhere in this book, I am always encouraged by repeated instances that come to my attention of church people who have been helped and healed completely on their own, so far as human aid is concerned. They possess sufficient faith and spiritual understanding to receive God's healing power. When their faith falters they offer the prayer of the father who brought his sick child to Jesus: "Lord, I believe; help thou my unbelief" (Mark 9:24).

A church member in one of my former parishes who has always been a leader among women shared with me the story of her deliverance from slavery to a habit-forming drug. Compelled to undergo an extensive stomach operation she was subject to a good deal of pain and had difficulty in sleeping. As a consequence her physician prescribed a drug. Unfortunately she became utterly dependent upon it and was steadily increasing the dose. According to her own testimony she would have been "petrified with fear" had she been asked to face a night without its aid.

Eight years after the first extensive surgery this woman had to

---

[6] *The Vital Balance*, p. 387.

undergo a second operation. The drugs then became even more important, entailing larger doses. She could not get through a single night without the aid of barbiturates and drugs. She had become an addict. Two years later she was reading in a religious journal when she happened upon an article concerned with faith in God. The author contended that by the exercise of faith and commitment to God and His purpose in our lives, miracles of deliverance can be wrought. There was nothing particularly new in the article except that it also dealt with the question of sleep. It pointed out that continuous sleep is not as important as some people think, that if one can learn to relax and let the mind dwell on helpful themes and especially if one can learn to receive the peace of God, it matters little whether or not there is a full night's sleep. She recalled that her own pastor had from time to time stressed this fact. The article, however, acted as a kind of catalyst. It brought things to a head. She resolved to try the experiment of a night without the drugs. She did it with fear and trembling. A verse from the Psalms (4:8) was a powerful aid: "I will both lay me down in peace, and sleep: for thou, Lord, only makest me dwell in safety." The thought of God and of His care for her and the peace that He puts into the hearts of His children induced sleep. She slept through the night. She slept the next night and the next. In short, after ten years of absolute dependence on drugs she was done with them forever. The shackles that had bound her were broken. She was free once more. She testified that if sometimes there may be an interval of wakening in the night, by thinking of God's presence and protection and quietly repeating to herself some well-loved Scripture passage she finds that she is rested and restored. "I am enjoying the best nights in my entire life," she concluded. The spiritual lift that she received from this experience is now standing her in good stead as she meets with life's inevitable times of testing.

While it is true that our Lord stressed emphatically the power of faith, there is no instance in the Gospels that I know of in which He ever blamed a sufferer for lack of faith. He did upbraid religious people for not manifesting more faith in God's healing power in the lives of others, but He dealt very tenderly with those who were sick. One of the cruelest things that some practitioners in the field of "faith healing" are sometimes guilty of is telling the sick person that he failed to recover because he lacked sufficient faith. That is a travesty on the teaching of Jesus and is often an "alibi" to cover the healer's failure. Our Lord never placed the onus for recovery on the sick person. This would only add the burden of guilt to the invalid's present distress. While He looked for faith in all who came to Him, rejoicing when He found it, He continued His mission of mercy in the most diverse situations. Oftentimes He healed even those persons who were completely bereft of hope.

Theologians of earlier centuries sometimes regarded the miracles of Jesus as a kind of a seal or proof of the authenticity of His person and His ministry. Not a few people in our time take the same view, as though our Lord needed something in addition to His incomparable life and teaching to validate His ministry. These remarkable healings, they think, were made to draw attention to Jesus and to personally exalt Him. They were His credentials to convince the doubting, testimonials to persuade the unbelieving. If we study the Gospel records, however, we shall see that they flatly contradict this viewpoint. Actually He shrank from publicity. Deliberately He sought to avoid the crowds. On more than one occasion He left the multitude that He might go alone into the mountain to pray. In the temptation in the wilderness Jesus completely rejected any thought of using startling or dramatic displays to win men to His Kingdom. The motivation for His healing lay in his all-consuming desire to make men whole and to bring them to God. If He were looking for the glorification of himself He never would have assured His followers that "greater works than these shall he do; because I go unto my Father" (John 14:12). He would have held back any transmission of power to the Apostles. His supreme motivation was an overwhelming compassion. Matthew makes this abundantly clear. "But when he saw the multitudes he was moved with compassion on them because they fainted and were scattered abroad as sheep having no shepherd" (Matt. 9:36). It was this unshepherded multitude of men and women to whom the compassionate heart of Jesus went forth in longing to heal, to restore, to redeem.

One of the most impressive characteristics in the life and ministry of Jesus is the impression one gets of inexhaustible reserve power. Jesus did not claim that this power originated in himself. He was the channel through which it flowed. He said, "The Father that dwelleth in me, he doeth the works" (John 14:10, AV). One of the most arresting illustrations of this power is found in the sixth chapter of Luke's gospel. In Phillips' translation we read: "It was in those days that he went up the hillside to pray, and spent the whole night in prayer to God. When daylight came, he summoned his disciples to him and out of them he chose twelve whom he called apostles. . . . Then he came down with them and stood on a level piece of ground, surrounded by a large crowd of his disciples and a great number of people from all parts of Judaea and Jerusalem and the coastal district of Tyre and Sidon, who had come to hear him and to be healed of their diseases. . . . The whole crowd were trying to touch him with their hands, for power was going out from him and he was healing them all" (Luke 6:12-13, 17, 19).

During that whole night in prayer Jesus was at the Fountainhead of all spiritual power and there He had drunk deeply of living waters. It was the power of the eternal God that issued from Him. How earnestly should everyone concerned with the healing of men and women ponder these words. He told His disciples that it was this power He was passing on to them. They too could become channels of divine energy.

This promise of the Master was undeniably fulfilled in the ministry of Christ's Apostles and followers whose deeds are recorded in the Book of Acts. Indeed to the end of the first century and beyond it the disciples of our Lord manifested in their healing ministry no diminishing of the divine power so constantly manifested in the life of the Master himself. It was after the first few centuries of Christianity that there came a tragic decline in the Church's ministry to the sick. This vital power we are seeking to regain in our time.

When Jesus was charged with casting out demons in the name of the prince of demons, He replied, "If it is by the finger of God that I cast out demons, then the Kingdom of God has come upon you" (Luke 11:20). It is this divine Kingdom or rule of God that Jesus came to proclaim. His healing ministry was one manifestation of the coming of this Kingdom. It would utterly transform the Church of Jesus Christ in our time if the leadership of the Church and its members in penitence and humility would seek a new and mighty manifestation of this Kingdom.

This Higher Order of God's rule from time to time breaks into our modern world and reveals its presence in the healing and transformation of men and women, but we have become so worldly wise today and so "scientific" in our thinking that oftentimes we are blind to great movements of the Spirit of God. We are so often forgetful of St. Paul's admonition: "Divine folly is wiser than the wisdom of man, and Divine weakness stronger than man's strength" (I Cor. 1:25, NEB).

Present-day Christians are in desperate need of the immeasurable power which is available to all of us in our human weakness. People who are faltering and failing would be given new purpose, new strength, and new visions of service to mankind would they but open their lives to the in-flowing power of God that was ever present in the life of Jesus. With such a consummation men would witness immeasurable divine energy in contact with measurable human need —the eternal love of Heaven healing the tragedies of earth.

"Preach the gospel, heal the sick." This is the mission that Jesus Christ gave to His disciples. How medicine, psychiatry, and religion, working in harmony, can bring a far larger measure of health to mankind is the theme of

DO YOU WANT
TO BE HEALED?
by John Sutherland Bonnell

Here is an important and strikingly different book on healing and the relation of the spiritual life to mental and physical illness.

DO YOU WANT TO BE HEALED? opens with a gripping account of the author's visit to the Shrine of Lourdes in France, famed site of purported miracles of healing, where both spiritual and medical factors in cures might be observed at work. He watched crowds of pilgrims and their sick in the hospital, the baths, the churches, and the all-important Grotto. He spent many hours at the Medical Bureau with internationally known medical scientists.

Dr. Bonnell also conferred on spiritual healing with religious and medical leaders on four continents, and sets forth the views of some present-day scientists. Drawing from his own records of more than 8,000 pastoral sessions, he cites many mental and physical healings which have been authenticated by physicians.